WEST
OF
REASON

Essays

D1523218

JONATHAN STEIN

For my grandfather

CONTENTS

ACKNOWLEDGMENTS

I would like to extend my sincere gratitude to Tarek Arafat for agreeing to be my editor. I contend without hesitation that his exuberance for life is unmatched and will remain immensely thankful for the ardor, incisive angles, and encouragement he brought to this project. And most importantly, the reminder that the shared nights of whiskey and writing can never possibly reach a surplus.

INTRODUCTION

F<small>ROM TIME TO TIME, UNKNOWINGLY OR PURPOSEFULLY, WE</small> all find ourselves in the grand audience of the history of ideas. The ones that compel you to stand up and pace around the room, scramble about to find a pen or pencil after throwing the book onto the floor, and rightfully distract from trivialities. In this way great ideas are like fierce surges of the wind, given that they are unavoidable and powerful forces of nature, and can alter direction and perspective with ease. Viewed in the aggregate, the ambition for writing the following pages can be traced back to the fusion of rigorous engagement with those perennial ideas and the craft that has preserved them for centuries.

In the early hours of inviting the start of the new decade (2020), I found myself last in a line of great company to give a toast to begin the year. In that moment I did not want to be precise, but instead as comprehensive as possible, to encapsulate *everything* in a short breath if I could. An all-encompassing phrase by Salman Rushdie bolted into my head and has yet to leave it, and I have since realized that it provides the proper beginning sentiment as to why I have composed this book. Other contenders would have fit as well, and are interspersed throughout the remaining sheets of paper, but only a few verses came to mind carrying the appropriate dosage of both gratitude of the moment and nostalgia for future ones:

> "Never forget that writing is as close as we get to keeping a hold on the thousand and one things—childhood, certainties, cities, doubts, dreams, instants, phrases, parents, loves—that go on slipping like sand through our fingers."

Life operates with a contingency that the recollection of these things will fall from memory. Arguably the best decision I have made was to start writing things down, which consciously served to organize thoughts but subconsciously acted in resistance to the former eventuality. To remember moments and ideas is to save them from oblivion. Over time I came to realize that this was not merely a flimsy exercise, and that the dialectic was not only inviting my attention but commanding it, with noticeable vibrancy. It was here that the fusion began to formulate. The amalgamation of writing and the study of an examined, meaningful, and enriched life gradually took its shape. The former passage lists the everyday fragments of life that are familiar to us all, and which are never absent in any argument despite not being immediately apparent upon first glance. Treasured bits of life are in every unexpected corner. It was an inescapable compulsion to be drawn to the debates that never die, alongside the virtues, reasons, and principles that seem indispensable in the scheme of existence. The subsequent pages consist of a selection of those ideas, knitted in the context of a grander purpose of which Rushdie also notes: to argue with the world.

Notable names in this effort are not always from the historical canon. Intriguing calls to action, rather than originate from the mouths of emperors or kings, can arise from offstage, as the quiet echo from the observer in the shadows. These are the declarations, I would argue, that can make more salient and lasting impressions. Poets are no more seated with this burden than others but seem to historically rise to the occasion. With a born affinity for the old world rather than the new, the tenor of W.H. Auden struck me as overwhelmingly fitting for the present moment. In his finest poem, "1 September 1939", he penned a lightning response to the invasion of Poland and the beginning to the second World War. As is the case with many great works, the reader is met with stanzas that could apply to both the past and present. Nearly a century later I would shamelessly like to resume where Auden left off, on the sentiment in his concluding expression of a mind lost in a country adrift:

Defenceless under the night / Our world in stupor lies;
Yet, dotted everywhere / Ironic points of light
Flash out wherever the Just / Exchange their messages:
May I, composed like them / Of Eros and dust,
Beleaguered by the same / Negation and despair
Show an affirming flame

Our cardinal position as a society has us west of reason, awaiting direction with a lack of both invigoration and wonder under Auden's night. I hope these essays might act as an invitation to a more rewarding confrontation with the world, a barefoot walk through the sands of existence listed by Rushdie. The essays are arranged in the order in which they were written with no other rhyme or reason beyond that. All in all, this short collection is merely a love letter to the reservoir of those grand ideas mentioned earlier, and the swashbuckling undertaking that follows to apprehend and ultimately employ them. Infinitely we are met with the great responsibility to patrol the corridors of judgment in the midst of chaos, to locate meaning in bedlam, and to continuously discover the composition to an enriched life. It is therefore a necessity to take our seats in that eternal audience—to live directly in contact with ideas, partitioning the convenient from the correct, with an urge to go on and create a new enlightenment.

DATA IN EVERYTHING

Fighting the current economic zeitgeist of indifference and intrusion

---

DAYS BEFORE THE GENERAL DATA PROTECTION REGULATION (GDPR) went into effect for the EU in late May of 2018, Mark Zuckerberg made a furtive move in the legal war room at Facebook. The multi-billion-dollar social media company used to be based in Ireland, mostly for tax purposes. If this were to have remained the case, all Facebook users would have fallen under the legal jurisdiction of GDPR: a regulation on data protection and privacy for citizens of the EU and the European Economic Area. This would have enabled the users of Facebook to fully understand how their data is leveraged *if* requested. Before the law went live and after it was approved by the European Parliament, Zuckerberg changed the structure of his organization to be domiciled in the United States instead. This evaporated the impending legal scrutiny from users who could have used the lever of the law to overturn the rocks of Facebook's privacy policies. Actions are necessarily tied to intent, and sometimes it is easier to unwrap the hidden objective of a given circumstance than one might hope. His act is transparently indicative of a new economic phenomenon. We live, to borrow the perfectly captured title of Shoshana Zuboff's book, in an age of surveillance capitalism — a profit-maximizing strategy for large corporations to collect and exploit private and personal information at the expense of all previous senses of liberty. The California Consumer Protection Act (CCPA), originally passed in September of 2018, is the first of its kind in the United States. With the legislation finally becoming effective at the turn of the decade, the first of January 2020, the reason why this law has been buried in the ether (when it should be on the front page of every newspaper in circulation) must be scrutinized.

Beneath the stratosphere that separates humankind from the unknown depths of space, a new form of dark matter has been steadily taking shape since the advent of digitized information. Big data has been designed to be undecipherable; even the term used to identify a pseudo location for it all, and by association, the orientation to which it lives relative to us, "the cloud", is designed to be enigmatic, deliberately out of reach, and on a higher plane of understanding. In a world where data is the engine behind so much commerce, it is remarkable how little we know about the full life cycle of our personal information. Who has it? What do they use it for? What is it *worth?* The level of uncertainty is alarming and becomes nefarious once the data careens into the personal realm. GDPR and CCPA were born out of those specific concerns and currently act as our only bulwark towards the excessive amount of data collection. Over time, personal identifiable information has become immeasurably lucrative for giant corporations. Our name, e-mail correspondence, credit card purchases, and countless other metrics have taken the form of all available particles and electromagnetic radiation that ends up lost in the vacuous black holes of Facebook, Google, Target, Amazon, Yahoo!, and many more companies.

These entities have pivoted from treating the public from consumers to the actual product. In turn, advertising agencies will buy our scraped data for improved accuracy with their ad-targeting. Now, future decision predictions are at the helm of the predictive algorithms. Consumer data is leveraged to direct users to desired outcomes and purchases using the poached information of private interests, hobbies, and history. And, as expected with any scam, companies market these behavioral futures as a positive element to consumerism in their long tirades of how our identities are being "understood". They argue our lives will become even more convenient once businesses such as their own know what we want before we do. Beneath the cacophony of framing bias and weak selling points, there is an undisputed allegiance to the profit motive.

A mainstream argument during the Age of Enlightenment dealt with social structures that could best preserve and protect both a republic government and human morality. Human behavior and motives were seen to change with stages of development for a society. The commercial society, the most advanced, was said to be the most susceptible to poison sacred values. Prevailing thought was that invitations to corruption and self-interest would usurp a sense of helping the public good. After stages of agriculture and pastorage, mankind changes. China is currently implementing a frightening exhibition of totalitarianism with their social credit scores based on camera surveillance and facial recognition technology. This level of extremism has not yet reached the West, where the current culture is one that, instead, offers a luxurious living experience allied with sumptuous commodities given by advanced commerce. It comes with the ability to live your life with an audience on social media and to have your online purchases selected *for* you rather than *by* you. In addition to the shift from enlightenment to entertainment (as Peter Thiel describes in his essay, "The Straussian Moment") there is enough to say that modernity represents the ingredients for the making of a cocktail specifically prepared to amuse ourselves to death.

As the shadow of this enterprise looms over more and more of our personal experience, our epistemology is directly warped as a consequence. Corporate giants in the private sector have been unilaterally tampering with our human agency without an invitation to do so. Our reality has become tailored to the calculated experience chosen for us grotesquely manifested in suggested advertisements, social media nudging, modified web search results based on location, and more. Initially appealing perhaps, but these companies aim to have us fooled by this psychological sleight of hand. What's next? Roger McNamee, a former adviser for Zuckerberg, starts with the knowledge that Google can tell we are human by the movement of our computer mouse. He asks, "What happens when my mouse movement becomes slower than it used to be, or becomes wobbly?" This is a logical leap to the next phase: if this can be proved indicative of a first sign of some disease like Parkinson's, the company that captures that data is under no obligation to tell the user. Without any penalties, insurance companies would undoubtedly be the first to snatch this information as the highest bidder, which could subsequently raise rates for the member or cut off coverage altogether. Even if it is falsely "diagnosed", these shady titans of industry have the ability to change the course of lives, without any reason to inform those affected.

The California Consumer Privacy Act is an empowering set of laws. The businesses that will be affected are 1) Companies with an annual gross revenue of more than $25 million, 2) companies that receive, share, or sell personal information of more than 50,000 individuals, and 3) businesses that earn 50% or more of their annual revenue from selling consumers' personal information. Consumers now have new license to exercise their "right to be forgotten". This involves the petition to have personal information deleted from data archives and to refuse the sale of this personal information to any third parties. After being pick-pocketed on a routine basis, consumers are now in the arena with the hustlers, able to fight against the theft of our own property.

Our society has always debated the trade-off between freedom and security, liberty and privacy. Historically the conversation has taken place in the public arena, but now it has shifted to the private sector. A marketplace is diverse because it's supposed to be unpredictable. Monopolies emerge when the freedom of choice is stripped from consumers, straying far from the model of theoretical perfect competition. Our economy and its main actors are not perfect by any means, but it is evident that certain businesses wish to carve their own version of a marketplace: one that is predictable, systematized, and controlled. The age of surveillance capitalism asks us to sacrifice freedom on the altar of convenience and human predictability, thereby placing a price on the most personal features to our being that were never for sale.

Imagine a slot machine that always lands on the winning spin combination — a device conceptualized and engineered by the so-called luminaries at the most recognizable corporations. It's an enticing product, but with a catch. The inputs to play are personal data, spending patterns, search engine history, and many more economic idiosyncrasies. The true incentives and the functional reasons behind the churning gears operating on the inside are cloaked from view of the user.

These corporations want the slot machines that predict human futures in the household of every American, and the CCPA forces the owners to unlock the panels to these data instruments and describe exactly how everything is maneuvered for their benefit, and why. As our laws continue to adapt to the uninvited level of involvement in our personal data, it will be because we will have remembered we never entered the casino in the first place.

THE PRICE OF WONDER

Deceit in the world of entertainment

THE GRAVE OF HARRY HOUDINI STANDS GENEROUSLY outspread at Machpelah Cemetery in Queens, New York. Photographs depict a statue of a woman in mourning seen kneeling beneath the bust of the famed illusionist, as well as playing cards peppered around his final resting place. Graveyards are mysterious scenes, vestiges of the remembered past. Death, it seems, is a concept that is intentionally hidden from the mobile parts of life. It is this way with the vast fields of land that contain the past performing hearts of loved ones, and the selection process for topics at the dinner table. Houdini entertained by bringing death onstage to masterfully elude it, which proved to be a magnificent draw for flocks of admirers all over the globe. Not only does his name survive, but his escape acts somehow transfigured it into its own form and description of slippery behavior. The elusive nature of Houdini's legacy still casts a silhouette representing matters of illusion and enchantment. A graveyard remains the ideal storybook setting for one to witness the presence of such notional ghosts, and the very real aura of the mystery of eternity. His grave site is regularly visited, as it so happens, with rituals that generate a pall of riddles and mystique. It is here, among the burial grounds of prior souls, that many paradoxes arise between the unbelievable and the believable, all best explored through the life of Houdini himself.

The Life and Afterlife of Harry Houdini

Two shadows followed Houdini throughout his life. They come intertwined in purpose, with a proneness to obsession and rigidness. The first—fame—is discussed in an investigation recently completed by Joe Pasnaski (in his new book with the above title) which reveals many misconceptions about the illusionist. According to an interview, the first and most astonishing perhaps is that Houdini was a rather incompetent magician. He once was so desperate he put out book out called "All I've Ever Learned about Handcuffs and Escape"—price on demand. Even before that, Houdini wholly embodied the stereotype of the struggling actor. He tried to make it in vaudeville, as a street performer, singer, and even a comedian for years. His big break came when he began performing drastic escape acts. With the lust for fame driving his work as he chased stardom, he eventually became lionized. Being the only performer at the time who was engaging with the style of escaping to a degree yet to be seen had its advantages. Henceforth, he deserved a league of his own. His acts increasingly flirted with danger, but once on a platform unreachable by his contemporaries, the concept of mortality traveled with him even beyond the protective dome of theater.

The most identifiable prop of a magician has to be the wand—the most powerless but powerfully garnished tool in existence. Despite knowing full well that brandishing such a wooden stick cannot produce direct effects upon the universe other than poking an eye out, it still carries the most value for sleight of hand gestures. Upon the death of a magician, a "broken wand ceremony" takes place during their funeral to symbolically indicate that the "magic has died with the man". One of these ceremonies still takes place at Houdini's final resting place every year. But this is rather redundant, is it not? Especially since obituaries for magicians typically read how they "outsmarted the soul and ensnared the senses" rather than "could literally walk on water". Perhaps not. . .

One of the stories that is told and retold about Houdini involves a woman who had her leg amputated toward the end of her life. Contacting her was compulsory for Houdini. This woman was relatively famous and he enjoyed chasing headlines. They started out as cordial acquaintances but gradually grew to be rather intimate friends. And after a while she had a request for Houdini: to please give her back her leg. In awe, but earnestly, he had to tell her that he has no real magical ability. He quipped, "I can only do the amazing, not the impossible."

Therein lies the great mystery of the world of magic—the fanciful realm of suspending the possible. Apart from feature films, magic is a spectacle that offers a glimpse into the fantasy of not only being able to defy the properties of matter and energy, but control them at will. Some people fundamentally believe that the natural order can be suspended by those who rise and fall under the very same laws of physics as their neighbor. Performances in this trade come in many forms, but all (usually) under the same assumption: that the audience is in on it. Crowds gather fully knowing the natural limit to human ability, but find it appealing to act as if the man on stage could levitate if he so desired. Everyone is supposed to know that being told we're in Oz is concomitant with the fact that there is a man behind the curtain.

The hackneyed Phaedrus expression, "Things are not always what they seem", has survived for centuries and would suffice here, but a more fitting locution might be: things are often *more* than they seem. The latter half of the quote is usually amputated from the former: ". . . the first appearance deceives many; the intelligence of a few perceives what has been carefully hidden." The hidden feature to Houdini's getaways were, more than anything, about cheating death. Death took a physical form in the steel can placed in the middle of Houdini's stage, filled to the brim with pails of water until it was overflowing. Rather inscrutably, Houdini would get handcuffed and climb inside. Tremors rippled throughout the audience as his head would disappear under water after the lid was enclosed and locked above him. Silence fell and eyelids stopped blinking. Unnerving as it may be, death is a subject worthy of iterative reflection before one arrives at the brink of paranoia. In "Aubade", a poem about death, Philip Larkin wrote of the sure extinction we all pretend to ignore, but to which Houdini volunteered his body:

> The mind blanks at the glare. Not in remorse
> — The good not done, the love not given, time
> Torn off unused — nor wretchedly because
> An only life can take so long to climb
> Clear of its wrong beginnings, and may never;
> But at the total emptiness for ever,
> The sure extinction that we travel to
> And shall be lost in always. Not to be here,
> Not to be anywhere,
> And soon; nothing more terrible, nothing more true.

Houdini arrived at a fundamental truth about the human condition while charming audiences with his act. Of his own free will, Houdini chose not only to face death but to make a fool out of it. What does it look like for someone to stare oblivion in the eye, and then avoid it? To escape mortality uses the most out of words like "spellbinding" and "beguiling". The concept of our own transience has immense power on where and how we direct our attention, and Houdini was one of the first iconic entertainers to realize it.

The very nature of Houdini's death is a testament to this phenomenon. Houdini's milk can escape is traditionally the prevailing thought as to how he died—a death defying act that went horribly wrong. He actually died a painfully banal death from appendicitis. It is incredibly likely that he invited his own demise by his challenge to have anyone punch him in the stomach without being (visibly) affected. A gentleman took his dare at an event and punched him multiple times before Houdini stopped him, and did not check himself into the hospital for days although in agonizing pain. He died five days later.

But what is memorable about that? It is almost as if history had to twist the circumstance, that a great man deserved a swan song equal to his success, to square the circle between fame and infamy. A quote from *The Lion in Winter*, perfectly rephrased by Aaron Sorkin for his former TV show, is suitable for this point. Three brothers are trapped and face execution. A dismissive comment comes from one of them: "As if it matters how a man falls down." To which another replies: *"When the fall is all that's left, it matters a great deal."*

Then: A Community of Faith

During his fame, Houdini had others threatening to share his stage of glory. While the proclivity to most folks interested in show business is to entertain others rather than cheat them, the world never quite seems to disappoint in appointing new ambassadors of fraud. Charlatans who exploited the harmless features of magic with an invidious motive filled the streets. These individuals, under many different titles such as "mediums" or "psychics", take the thematic structure to magic—an experience with the unknown—and cash in for their personal gain at the expense of the credulity of the public. And yet the very nature of their hoax is self-evident by the sheer outcomes, or lack thereof, of their proclaimed talents. There's a reason why hospitals don't employ faith healers and psychics have yet to be seen directing war strategies. The flip side to the world of entertainment via innocuous magic is a community of hucksterish con men and women who seem to care for all the right things for all the wrong reasons.

Spiritualism was at its height during the early 20th century. Scores of mediums, fortune tellers, and astrologists were consulted on the afterlife. They claimed, as their successors still do, that they had a gift to communicate with the spirits of those who had already left the earth. The movement had a very famous advocate—Arthur Conan Doyle—and as it turns out, many other prominent figures with a public life. A bill was introduced in Congress in 1926 that would have inflicted a $250 fine or six months in prison for "any person pretending to tell fortunes for reward or compensation" in the District of Columbia. Houdini campaigned and testified for this bill and saw to it that he exposed clairvoyants for their fraudulent and manipulative lifestyle. In the process, it was discovered that this was a fool's errand. Many leading public figures in Washington, along with their families, took psychic divination incredibly seriously.

It was no secret that Florence Harding, the wife of our 29th President, regularly sought the predictions from mediums in the White House. With this topic on the national stage it was discovered that seances were still held during the Coolidge administration. Apparently, this extended to many members of Congress as well. The extent of it was revealed during the public debate over the subject. Senators and representatives began to make unabashedly sincere and pathetic assertions about their beliefs. Representative Ralph Gilbert from Kentucky, clearly bothered by Houdini's apparent haughty demeanor, even went so far as to declare his belief for fairies and Santa Claus.

The serious criticisms to Houdini's disdain for apparent celestial connections were arguments that seeking paranormal guidance was a principle of their religion. There still was a blaring case of separation of church and state to be argued here, not to mention a fundamental difference in the manifestation of religious prerogative. Houdini saw this pervasive psychic influence on Capitol Hill as a dangerous consideration to the governing abilities of the men and women who actively received advice from those who sell nonsense for a living. Quite correct, of course, as the unnerving nature of how those in power make their decisions became prudent once again just years ago when President Reagan's former Chief of Staff revealed how Reagan used to consult with astrologers and use their predictions to aid his domestic and international options. As this is unstable at best and utterly mortifying at worst, the public outrage was rightfully earned when the news broke. These flippant displays in the White House should really be deemed interregnums.

Houdini even employed a spy to uncover and reveal how mediums would feign their supernatural power. Her name was Rose Mackenburg. She was known for her elaborate costumes allied with cunning acting schemes to trick supposed psychics into divulging information that would deem them frauds. She compiled a mountain of evidence in favor of skepticism that today would be used as companion pieces for the grand larceny suits that are replete against mediums. Her findings were used to support Houdini's case in 1926, but once again were futile in the end with a clergy of congressional apologists for ghost whisperers.

Now: Contemptible Predators

"Kayfabe" is a term used in professional wrestling as a type of code to describe the manufactured simulation that takes place in the squared circle. Although the fans that tune in are mostly aware that the outcomes are predetermined and are purely the sake of entertainment, it clearly does not matter. Research by evolutionary biologists suggests that mendacity rather than pure transparency is more efficient at playing the decisive role in systems of environmental change. Essentially, it is more likely that we create a certain mass of falsehoods from true information that directly contribute to how high or low we want to calibrate our attention towards a certain thing. A passage from Robert Trivers in *The Folly of Fools* describes the cognitive operations:

> "We seek out information and then act to destroy it. On the one hand, our sense organs have evolved to give us a marvelously detailed and accurate view of the outside world … Together our sensory systems are organized to give us a detailed and accurate view of reality, exactly as we would expect if truth about the outside world helps us to navigate it more effectively. But once this information arrives in our brains, it is often distorted and biased to our conscious minds. We deny the truth to ourselves … We repress painful memories, create completely false ones, rationalize immoral behavior, act repeatedly to boost positive self-opinion, and show a suite of ego-defense mechanisms."

The truth is sprawled out, clear as day. Illusionists are not *really* claiming that they can walk on water. These days, professional wrestling is not *really* claiming that these athletes are out for blood. Psychics, mediums, and fortune tellers, however, *do claim* that they have special abilities that most humans do not possess. For this reason, they do not operate under the full assumption of "kayfabe", but rather engage in transparent chicanery to trick the audience with their gag. According to Trivers, our pattern and frequency for self-deception is the perfect catalyst companion for their game. Magic is one of the few disciplines that value deception as an art, but a line has to be drawn.

Whistle-blowers within the industry have explained how it all works. Psychic hotlines implore their workers to keep callers on the phone as long as possible, being paid by the minute. They are also taught how to extract as much personal information as possible to aid their forecasts at the end. Some organizations even go as far as fulfilling their own predictions, such as foreseeing a "future threat" which results in the company mailing death threats to the caller inciting them to call their personal psychic for guidance on how to avoid their ultimate demise. These individuals regrettably never get the press of someone like Bernie Madoff or Charles Keating. It is much easier to defame people completely devoid of care for your finances, but the same rule of ridicule must apply when the product is invisible. As with every positive claim, the burden of proof remains on the sycophants within the psychic universe to demonstrate their gifts. A committee for Scientific American, for which Houdini was a member, offered a substantial cash prize for any medium who was able to prove their supernatural abilities. All participants either could not produce evidence or were found guilty of cheating, even by third party investigations. The door is still open. . .

Looking On

It is reasonable to inquire why Houdini did not add psychic powers to his arsenal. After all, he was consumed with the idea of fame and wanted to remain an incomparable international icon. A fair-minded deduction would be to say that he was a conscious arbiter of the ethical line in his profession. Individuals actively seek out mediums in times of incredible uncertainty. It is only natural to want to ascribe reasons to unthinkable tragedies, and to look out into the void for answers. A conversation with the beyond is warranted; the hunt persists for a dialogue that extends beyond the outer rims of our galaxy. But sometimes there is silence (ghostly described by Nietzsche as the gradual realization of the abyss staring back at you if you were to gaze for too long). The desire to defy these harsh realities is perfectly within the nature of being human, independent of religious belief.

In all fairness, some people just want to know what tomorrow will hold. The true numeric figure of those who believe their fortune cookie is literally true, along with their horoscope in the newspaper, is somewhat unknown. (As a quick aside on the mention of astrology—it should be much easier to search for the circulation of public scorn this superstition deserves. Even gentle humor can effectively knock this solipsistic belief out of orbit, as in the case of an editor who had been instructed to pen the termination letter for the writer of the newspaper's astrology column. The letter began by saying, "As I have no doubt you will have foreseen . . .") Any which way, an external locus of control creates a desire to not be surprised about the cruelness that nature can inflict upon anyone. However, those who claim to have a connection with the afterlife, or a crystal ball that see into the future, parade around playing to these vulnerable inclinations. As professional swindlers, they combine the harmless elements of magic and exploit the susceptible fragments of the human psyche.

The utility of the concept of nothing, of uncertainty, and fear can be used in many facets. Houdini used it to his advantage with his unprecedented escape acts to pull off "the amazing". But he never lied about the impossible.

THE PERFECT ALIBI

How the realm of fiction has a Janus-faced identity

NOVEMBER 22ND, 1963—A CLEAR MORNING GREETED THE
president and his wife on a routine political trip to Texas. This
unseasonably warm Friday afternoon in Dallas that was
destined to be ordinary now lives in infamy. The assassination
of JFK has all of the purposefully ambiguous and peculiar
components for the making of one of the greatest conspiracy
theories in history. The question of the man with the umbrella,
the number of gunshots heard, the Babushka lady, medical
evidence from Kennedy's body, his driver's odd reaction—all
perfectly mysterious enough to make one wonder if the world
is really aware of the truth about what happened that fateful day.
Thousands of books have been written about the incident based

on the idea that the act of a lone gunman named Lee Harvey Oswald is almost too simple an explanation.

The same class of thinking is home to even more tales that seem wrenched from a lucid dream rather than the chronicle of history. There's the conspiracy theory that Hitler escaped to Argentina, that beneath the Denver airport is the covert city headquarters for the New World Order, and the belief that the Beatles never even existed. Is it even remotely possible to rate these perilous ideas on a spectrum of impossibility? Stranger things have happened . . .

CIA: Conspiracy in Action

Ten years prior to the JFK assassination, the world was witnessing the dawn of the Cold War. The United States and Russia were to engage in a series of proxy wars until the early 1990's in relentless hegemonic races. These battles would include the competition in space, nuclear proliferation, and many other dangerous feats. An international whisper began to circulate that the Soviets were engaged in developing and enhancing their means of psychological warfare. There were already accounts of their methods from WWII from prisoners of war, but these rumors were of a different breed of torture. It was believed that the Soviets were involved in mind control experiments, as well as concocting "truth serum". Lastly, and most importantly, there was word that the Soviets had gotten their hands on a new drug, lysergic acid diethylamide (LSD), and were experimenting with methods to weaponize the use of it. The United States responded like a toddler learning that their sibling just got a new toy. Without much investigation into these claims, the Central Intelligence Agency quickly saw implications that caused ripples of fear. State secrets could be spilled easily if agents became under the influence of this drug, America would be out-hustled in obtaining the mastery of this new torture formula without understanding how to combat it, and the Soviets would surely utilize their knowledge as political negotiating leverage. It would be like giving the devil his spear. LSD was only a pharmaceutical at this particular moment in history. First synthesized in 1938 by a Swiss chemist named Albert Hofmann, the effects of the compound were mostly unknown. A Swiss pharmaceutical company, Sandoz Pharmaceuticals, had millions of hits of LSD on the open market. The CIA bought *all of them*.

Drunk on the limitless possibilities and armed with (literally) buckets full of LSD, the program that would later become infamous and haunt the legacy of the organization was initiated: MKUltra. To define the scope of the project is difficult due to the wide-reaching impacts, but there were a few overarching goals: (a) Discover the effects of LSD and its capacity to contribute to mind-control techniques to battle the Soviets; (b) Gain exploratory insight into the possibility of utilizing the drug to carry out assassinations of foreign leaders; (c) Acquire new knowledge and experience regarding psychological torture.

Rapidly, the CIA carefully constructed testing centers with controlled environmental factors. Renowned doctors and psychologists were consulted to ensure the safety measures of the operation were ironclad, and there was substantial transparency between the government and the public on the methods behind their investigative project. Or, so you would expect.

The Doors to Hell

Instead, the final choice for the test subjects for this dangerous and "Most Secret" level program was none other than unsuspecting citizens of the American public. This is not an instance of hyperbole. The CIA—an intelligence agency dedicated to the protection of American citizens—secretly dosed ordinary people across the country by means of LSD without their expressed or implied consent.

The footprint of the CIA was everywhere. They entered prisons, drug-infested neighborhoods, even a veterans hospital to perform their experiments. The unabated conduct toward negligence of (what should seem) innate morality during the trial was unforeseeable. One unlucky Kentucky-based patient was continuously dosed for 174 days straight. They approached heroin addicts and enticed them to take LSD by trading them with more heroin in return. Magicians were brought in to teach operatives how to use sleight of hand to slip anything into the drinks of their desired target. Armed with their undercover personas and a new psychedelic drug, the CIA had their hands around the throats of unwitting victims across the country.

The CIA rented "pads" out in San Francisco for subsidiary projects, the most famous being "Operation Midnight Climax". Parties would be hosted at these venues in the current hippie district of the city with everyone invited eventually tripping (and mostly unknowingly) on LSD. One particular house had a two-way mirror for the experimenters to hide behind and observe as the chaos unfolded. Stories of civilized men and women becoming utterly unrecognizable were replete in the reports. Understandably so, since this was at a time when the correct dosage for an individual was still relatively unknown. One U.S. Marshal even tried to rob a bar after attending one of these parties. Perhaps the most infamous case during this initiative was that of Frank Olsen. Nine days after he was unwittingly subjected to the perils of an unknown drug, he threw himself out the window of his hotel in NYC. Although ruled as a suicide, his body revealed signs of intense bruising that were not the result of the fall. If he didn't jump on his own volition, the implication of foul play arises. What exactly happened here? And why? It is currently an unsolved case as to how Frank Olsen, a married man, and a father to three children, ultimately met his end. . .

After the conclusion of WWII, the United States was instrumental in organizing the Nuremberg code: a set of international laws on the limits of human experimentation in response to the horror seen by the Germans during the

Holocaust. There were ten points to the code, and although it could be argued that the CIA violated all ten, they were most certainly responsible for completing ignoring the following seven supposed injunctions:

1) The voluntary consent of the human subject is absolutely essential.

2) The experiment should be so conducted as to avoid all unnecessary physical and mental suffering and injury.

3) The degree of risk to be taken should never exceed that determined by the humanitarian importance of the problem to be solved by the experiment.

4) Proper preparations should be made and adequate facilities provided to protect the experimental subject against even remote possibilities of injury, disability, or death.

5) The experiment should be conducted only by scientifically qualified persons. The highest degree of skill and care should be required through all stages of the experiment of those who conduct or engage in the experiment.

6) During the course of the experiment the human subject should be at liberty to bring the experiment to an end if he has reached the physical or mental state where continuation of the experiment seems to him to be impossible.

7) During the course of the experiment the scientist in charge must be prepared to terminate the experiment at any stage, if he has probable cause to believe, in the

> exercise of the good faith, superior skill and careful
> judgment required of him that a continuation of the
> experiment is likely to result in injury, disability, or death
> to the experimental subject.

Not even ten years after the world witnessed perhaps the most egregious offense to humanity in history, the United States government decided to blatantly flout the doctrine written to ensure something of the same kind would never be repeated.

This was not the only instance of going beyond the pale for the CIA in the fifties and beyond. Despite a few patches of success, the agency has a record with the appearance of a resumé dipped into a pot of frightening imperialism and startling human rights violations. After the second world war, the bountiful arms of the agency reached out to a *thousand* Nazi war criminals and offered them employment. Among them was General Reinhard Gehlen, who oversaw the entirety of German-based intelligence operations for Hitler. These realizations were unearthed by Congress many years ago, and perhaps the elapsed time has tainted an equivalent response. Under his direction, these retired officers of the Third Reich were, according to a report, ". . . *instrumental in helping thousands of fascist fugitives escape via 'ratlines' to safe havens abroad—often with a wink and a nod from U.S. intelligence officers.*" The CIA was additionally involved in the overthrow of democratically elected leaders of Guatemala (Jacob Arbenez) and Iran (Mohammad Mossadegh) in back-to-back years. Also included in these plots was the round-up assistance of dissenting figures trying to stymie their insurgency efforts, such as the revolutionary Che Guevara. All of these atrocities, and many more, get rolled up to a title of a government agency that mandates the notion of secrecy for its support and enforcement. The alluring nature of "covert" and "classified" are unhealthy labels that keep the public in a state of reverence, but conveniently requires nothing to earn it.

So, naturally, the records of MKUltra were not ones that the government wanted anyone to ever see. In 1973, the director of the CIA ordered a complete purge of all documents related to the project. They nearly succeeded in the complete destruction of everything—from the numerous stacks of records to the staples and paper clips that held them together—but 20,000 pages accidentally survived. They were misfiled in a financial cabinet. Years later they were found, and the entire secret enterprise was exposed.

It begs the question: what if these documents had made it to incinerator? We would have thousands of individuals scattered throughout the U.S. all claiming the same thing: a main reason for their erratic behavior and depression was that during the 50's and 60's, they and others had been unwittingly drugged by their own government and the affects were still haunting them.

Would we believe them?

Would *you* believe them?

The Origin of Doubt

It is rather puzzling to imagine exactly why conspiracy theories form and what prompts them to crystallize. They all begin someplace — take the New World Order conspiracy for example. The basis for someone to believe that a select group of international elites are in complete control of the operations of the World Bank, the EU, and the global media could come from anywhere. But fundamentally it begins with a distrust in all of the systems, institutions, and individuals designed to exhibit the truth about a given circumstance. And sometimes a general skepticism toward those entities are warranted. Doubt fuels investigation. But when something rational (the proclivity for those in power to lie) is then used to conclude something irrational (the entire world is out to deceive you), a fundamental problem arises. These theories are desperately trying to complete an outlandish syllogism to fit their narrative. And now, when it should seem obvious that these claims should not be awarded a megaphone, there are instances like this one that make the self-evident more difficult to defend.

Standing on its own, MKUltra sounds fictional. It sounds like the plot to the next Stephen King novel, or a pitch to a production company for the blockbuster horror film coming next spring. Unfortunately, the CIA does not necessarily engage in mundane work, and therefore has a history of other morally questionable practices that could dilute the overall surprise of this initiative. If so, it is even more evident that we are accustomed to turning a blind eye toward institutions that are designed to keep us safe. Even if they suddenly turn on us. If some employee or agent had gotten an extra hour of sleep and filed the incriminating documents in the pile labeled, "PLEASE BURN IMMEDIATELY", the MKUltra story would be indistinguishable from any other conspiracy theory. The only reason that it might seem less insane than other postulations is merely because we have the benefit of knowing it to be true.

And that's the problem here — what the hell are we supposed to do when claims that seem so nonsensical, so implausible, so downright fictitious that we dismiss the thought of it before it fully forms? It shouldn't lend credence to beliefs of the same ilk, but it should raise suspicions and standards. Otherwise, those with great power can hide behind the cloak of impossibility forever. Especially if we are going to, as it seems, live with an institution that has the prerogative to disregard the rule of law so that we can accumulate and process foreign intelligence to prevent attacks on our land and partake in foreign government operations.

Discovering the appalling nature of MKUltra should not prompt the purchase of a book outlining an alternate theory to the JFK assassination, or further research into other fanciful claims for that matter. At the very least it should tame and re-calibrate the classification of conspiracies. Most crucially, it sharpens the perception of what the worst injustices look like: perverse irony. Priests who molest children. Spouses who vow to monogamy and then cheat. Institutions that claim to function for your protection that suddenly assault you. The bad actors of the world rely on the supposition that nothing could be otherwise, and exploit it to the detriment of those who believe people have good intentions and not deplorable ones. They are afforded an alibi when under the protection of some cultural or societal monolith. Petrifying moments in history occur under these circumstances, when something that seems like a conspiracy theory suddenly becomes real.

BRIDGES FROM A POET

Beauty and allure in the face of calamity

AS EVERYONE ACROSS THE GLOBE TAKES THE SAME PRACTICAL
directions to combat this invidious pandemic, there has been
substantial conversation about how to value life as we once
knew it. Engaging in the drudgery of each working day and
perfunctory social platitudes now seem like pure luxuries. Not
that there wouldn't be, but there really is something strange
about the civilized world screeching to a halt. The obvious
reasons are evident. Humanity is a batch of social animals that
extensively rely on interaction with others. The others might be
more subtle but are placidly awaiting our attention. As we draw
the curtains on each other for a while, musings and questions of
what is pleasing, what is valuable, and what is *beautiful* about
life are pressing against the frontier of our thoughts.

The stock price of everything mundane, to begin, seems to have appreciated significantly. Going to a coffee shop, the hum of nature, and perhaps even the obligation to shave are all surely missed. But the value of all *nuisances* seem to be behaving the same way. The sirens from the street late at night, for instance, or the indecisiveness between friends as lunch plans become as difficult as cracking the Enigma code, are no longer occurring at the moment. One of the only positives to emerge from the coronavirus is that it has refined the previous elements to life. With the world on pause right now, we are all experiencing what could very well be a long interruption to aspects originally thought to be invariable. When society returns to its collective busyness, the very same routine features to life will be present. Hopefully they will capture our attention more than before.

Beyond the unwavering parts to life, the next sphere of occurrences are typically thought of as inherently pleasurable events and milestones: concerts, graduations, weddings and other celebrations of talent and accomplishments. As the circle around everything in life expands to encompass everything we have and will experience, from the everyday stimuli to the scattered bits of enjoyment, we are eventually left with existence itself. In these times especially, it's rather automatic to reflect with some disdain on the nature of things. Perhaps not to the extreme of the few prominent members of the antinatalism community who believe life is truly not worth living, but an urge to curse at life can be unavoidable at times. Regrettably, we are witnessing an aggressive infectious agent run the earth. There have been unnecessary deaths caused by the coronavirus, scores of events that have been canceled or postponed, and the world economy has been in free fall for nearly a month. It's possible in one moment to value the mundane parts to life higher than we did before. In the next, we are keenly aware of the stunning absurdity—that a nearly invisible particle containing nucleic acid has caused the entire globe to stop what its doing. Cabin fever is creeping up from behind as everyone attempts to square this circle.

On the other side of the spectrum from everything mundane is everything magnificent and beautiful. The pleasing of the senses or mind is the general thought to define beauty, along with the idea that it is subjective, which has always been an irritable part of its definition and contributes to its incompleteness. Beauty has a seduction and magnetism that makes it *seem objective*. Features and creations exist, both natural and contrived, that can be seen as objectively delightful but fail to pass the tests of moralism and universality. The sunset, for example, or perhaps music, or certain human achievements. But the blind have no means to appreciate the sunset, as well as individuals suffering from xeroderma pigmentosum: a genetic disease which causes severe sensitivity to the eyes and skin from ultra violet light, and those who are deaf cannot reap the listening pleasure of Beethoven's symphonies. The milestones listed before are also flawed. Not everyone receives an education, and not everyone is fortunate enough to find a "soulmate". Even other aesthetic treasures are not *by nature* purely without suffering. The ocean for instance, in the same moment of being a dazzling spectacle, holds the bodies of those who have drowned at sea. In the depths of each major body of water is a slugfest between the powerful and meek members of the food chain. Not to mention, the ocean has the potential (as it has done in the past) to rise up and reveal the extent of its stature and capability, and demolish the towns of those near it and the lives of those close enough to be in its way. For any elegant feature to life, from mountains and vistas to love and laughter, there are conditions that prevent certain individuals from appreciating them in full and even are the direct cause of tragedy rather than euphoria. The question becomes: Is real beauty actually concerned with morality? Not in all judgments, but the highest rung of world order does require an imperative to maintain a level of honor and intellectual health for humanity. Kant, for instance, writes of a concept that says certain moral obligations are *unconditional* that he calls the "categorical imperative". To borrow his classification, there does seem to be an aesthetic imperative to experiences as well.

So, we stand trapped in the amber of the moment, as Kurt Vonnegut would submit. Subjective beauty is unavoidable but can be thought of in terms separate from traditional impulses. Something can be beautiful *because* it's broken. Everything is flawed somehow, with human beings as the prime example. Beauty can live in the fleeting moments, the ones that are unable to be replicated, and the things that don't last forever. The only source, it seems, in which no substitutes may be offered on the aesthetic dimension of judgment comes from "Ode on a Grecian Urn", a poem by John Keats who, with immense courage, offered two highly contested remarks in poetry to conclude one of his famous pieces. The last few lines read as follows:

> When old age shall this generation waste,
> Thou shalt remain, in midst of other woe
> Than ours, a friend to man, to whom thou say'st,'
> "Beauty is truth, truth beauty,—that is all
> Ye know on earth, and all ye need to know."

In the midst of this pandemic, it is more evident than ever before that truth is the singular force of unity in the belly of chaos; something that we can't touch or see but only understand. It discriminates against no one and renders direction and knowledge. Although our epistemology is frequently fuddled with lies, the truth should always remain our constant pursuit. It leads to the interrelation between the two ascriptions and the concession that the highest pillar of beauty must align with virtue and be infallible, something that never fails.

When uncertainty is the towering standard, beauty can be easily obfuscated. Art can be thought of as opposite to facts, but this is a false antithesis in many ways. Veracity in the world will always remain if one is ever disoriented in the search for what is beautiful — but the final layer of the intrinsic experience has to come from a permanent origin, unyielding to the imagination. To live in reality and contiguity is therefore always a particle of beauty. It evicts all attempts to misconstrue or knavishly warp one's vision of what is real. The two properties posed by Keats can exist in tandem without either being dependent on the other. This occurs more frequently than is noticeable, but additional time spent as observers can provide the space to reflect on when and how this manifests. Everything, including and especially our own transience, remains as beautiful as it was before.

I CAN'T BREATHE: AN EVOLUTION OF THOUGHT

The resurgence of an undying historical plight

(These passages by no means exhaust all of the important arguments that have erupted over the last few months. They are selections of various thoughts and rebuttals to the events of the political movement, in a form of personal reflection but serious commentary.)

Wednesday, May 27ᵗʰ

THOSE OF US ALREADY AGAINST CAPITAL PUNISHMENT usually find our way to the opinion by the idea that the state should not kill people. These gruesome occurrences come in the case of Ricky Ray Rector — the Bill Clinton controversy — where the subjects are led to their execution behind closed doors and out of sight from society, or in broad daylight in the middle of Minneapolis.

George Floyd is not the first and certainly won't be the last victim of police brutality in America. A few years ago, the country heard "I can't breathe" for the first time from the mouth of Eric Garner, a New York resident who was choked to death by an officer on Bay Street in Staten Island. The outcry was heard on the international microphone again on Monday night from Mr. Floyd in yet another obscene act of unnecessary violence from those who supposedly enforce the law. Continuously, it seems, we can rely on instances of egregious and unbridled behavior from the police on the black community. Their constitution turns physical, their resolve becomes excessive, and the price is paid in catastrophic losses of life which never match the mediocre transgressions.

Both instances were initiated on the prospect of the type of criminality that hardly begets the blink of an eye, especially when contrasted with the resolution of their lives. Garner was supposedly selling illegal cigarettes and rumors were attached to Floyd about a bogus $20 bill. Upon the initial confrontation, both men reportedly resisted arrest. The Garner case has recorded evidence of his words before he was pummeled by four officers. His assertion comes in the form of just a few sentences, all the while pleading his innocence, demonstrating civility, and referring to the officer with respect. He immediately raised his hands to signal surrender once the charge at him began, when he was treated like a beast rather than a man, with his further exclamation coming moments later in the same gasps for air as George Floyd: "I can't breathe".

Garner was held in a chokehold for fifteen seconds by Daniel Pantaleo before his face was needlessly shoved into the pavement. In a seemingly draconian and pathetic drive to upstage Pantaleo, Floyd's attacker held his knee on his neck for nearly ten minutes while he was on the ground screeching for oxygen until he eventually lost consciousness. This is so revolting, foul, and unambiguous that it has crowded out all potential space for nuance of police tactics involved in the discussion. Two things are certain. The first is that the methods of retaining these men were grossly overdone. The second is that resisting arrest, especially for such small grievances, should not be equally countered by the threat of death. On the matter of resisting arrest, those who argue that nothing further would have ensued if these men hadn't done so seem to be portraying the traits of our primate species that are more ape than human. Nobody should have to worry about their own life until they credibly threaten the life of another.

The officer, Derek Chauvin, who used his knee to actively suffocate Mr. Floyd was immediately fired whereas the officer who choked Mr. Garner wasn't fired *until five years after the incident.* At least it's progress of a kind, but the imbalance of it all was acutely noted by comedian John Cleese. He sarcastically commented that since he is a self-employed person, he wonders if he could murder someone in exchange for a promise to fire himself. Although this is not the end of the punishments in the Floyd case, it remains possible that it could be. The grand jury investigation did not result in any indictment for the Garner case, after all. I do, however, expect and duly hope for proportional retribution for George Floyd and his family. Any sort of retaliatory threat had been neutralized with his hands cuffed and face thrust into gravel. This was a homicide.

While we await the final verdict, we are left with the haunting moments of George Floyd's last breath as he was pinned against the asphalt. Other citizens stood nearby, objecting to the conduct of the officer. In his last moments, George Floyd heard his bystanders implore the officer to stop by attempting to appeal to his humanity, asking for a pulse check, and repeating his outcry for him. This was all they could do, frankly speaking. It is inconceivable to ask for any more heroism or remonstrance from people who were seeing the law blatantly ignored in front of them. They could have been next. Through their objections, Mr. Floyd was able to see the genesis of the earnest and stark fear that is spreading across the country. The witnesses of this heinous act gave him a glimpse of what is to come, hopefully, in the form of justice. The only dignified reflection to come from this horrifying display of evil was that in his last moments, George Floyd was able to look protest in the eye.

Friday, May 29th

America, it seems, had no patience left. The streets are full, and demonstrations have ensued. I could not have expected the protests to intensify to this degree. My core reaction is a mixed sensation of pride and consternation. To live in a country in which such an eruptive reaction to the murder of a handcuffed black man is allowed by our blanket of freedom is of paramount importance. Many people have notably combed through history and pointed to many other marches and rallies that were catalysts for change. And as racism continues to plague our massively advanced but divided nation, these protests are a physical reaction from us trying to push this anachronistic mindset out of this generation and into the void.

There is something, however, immensely alarming right now. The police, day after day and night after night, have been caught on camera attacking *plainly innocent and defenseless people.* Members of the media have been shot at with rubber bullets, tear gas has been used against those who are armed with nothing, and assaults from officers have ranged from using their fists to their cars. One reporter likened what he has seen to riots in China and Iran. This problem has been videotaped and commented on before in the past few decades, but now the malady is unavoidable. Police brutality is pestilent and without excuse. There have also been extreme measures taken by those promoting the idea of equality, which is in direct opposition to the cause and only destructive. On the other hand, there have been far too many cases of the police simply ignoring looters that many are excluding from their judgment. Pure instinct promotes the thought that the peace inhibitors within these individuals have simply cracked. They've witnessed systematic oppression and subjugation for too long and can only take so many blows to their identity and fellow man. Although property destruction is completely unnecessary, it's also a signal. Sheer disbelief from the gallery awaits anyone who attempts to argue that property is worth more than a human life.

The third-degree murder charge for Chauvin is, in my opinion, not sufficient. The definition by the Minneapolis Legislature begins by saying, "Whoever, without intent to effect the death of any person..." which has already inadequately comprised the full extent of the case. When an individual engages in an act that (by all reasonable accounts) can kill someone, they have forfeited all rights to speculate about their intent. Here, the law must reside on the side of the victim. And kneeling on the esophagus of another human being for nearly ten minutes is well within a reasonable definition for intent to kill. Otherwise, we are going to find ourselves on a slippery slope of impunity when people who are arrested for shooting someone in the stomach say they weren't trying to kill, because if they had been then they would have aimed for the head.

Chauvin is not the only guilty party. The other three officers present should not be exonerated. In *On Liberty*, John Stuart Mill had this to say on moral liability: "A person may cause evil to others not only by his actions *but by his inaction, and in either case he is justly accountable to them for the injury.*" Applying this practically will mostly involve a murky conclusion. Here, in Minneapolis, it seems all too clear. (A separate note: this level of ethics is notably difficult to exhibit, which is all the more reason one should keep it on their conscious.) By now, this idea has become easily digestible. The abuse in the streets from cops invokes enough panic to cause a riot within yourself, as the great Pakistani writer Rafia Zakaria noted. The elderly have been mauled down, men and women are now blind from being blasted in the eye with rubber bullets, and cops have beat peaceful protesters with such force that you would think they had just found their child's kidnapper. We have watched other officers stand by like a cretinous pack of wolves as one of their own torments its prey. None of this seems to be occurring to the vandalizers and destructors themselves, only to those standing in solidarity, which further promotes a thought of political and racial bias. The illegality is staggering, but vital to watch to feel the residual pain of the country.

Tuesday, June 2

Yesterday evening the District had an ambience to it that, I believe, would even make residents feel like strangers in their own neighborhood. The streets were blocked off and people simply seemed on alert. There was no feeling of business or commerce, but rather an empty town that had lost its face.

Protesters were bellowing and chanting around the corner, pressed against the closest fence to the White House. A line of officers stood about twenty-five feet back on the lawn in Lafayette Park with protective shields. The scene was something out of a backward action film that had somehow confused the parts of the heroes and villains. The cops stood with their backs defending the home of this crooked administration as choruses of impeachment and corruption rang from the crowd. We chanted the names of those who had lost their lives, admonishment of reprieves, and other cries of heartbreak for those who couldn't any longer.

Movement began in the distance. Trucks carrying the National Guard rolled in from the left, and they gradually made their way to the front lines to extend the human wall. This stream of reinforcements didn't end for a full hour and before we knew it there were several hundred officers facing the crowd. Our assembly, too, was growing. We were forced closer together and the chants grew louder. Then, after no means of violence or disruption of any kind, we saw what can only be described as deliberate engagement preparation. Slowly but surely, each officer was handed gas masks and guns. They transformed from officers to soldiers. The leisurely way in which this was conducted was quite petrifying. A look of bewilderment swept across the crowd as we attempted to grapple with the reasonable world we used to know and the one we were witnessing in front of us. The power imbalance slowly heightened, the uncertainty of what was about happen escalated, and the tension that was once suspended in the air shifted to everyone's chests.

Before we had the choice to stay or leave, we lost our footing as surges of protesters began to retreat from our left. Although we didn't know why at the time, authorities had begun clearing a path for Trump to walk to St. John's church a few blocks away. Mace and flash bombs were thrown our way based on no signs of instigation from our end. On the news later we would see, yet again, unnecessary aggression towards the media and peaceful citizens amid the ensuing chaos. There was nothing left to be done after the police utilized tear gas, which is banned in international warfare and multiple global treaties, and deliberately created unrest by their ferocity. The rest was to be observed on the news. After returning home, we learned of Trump's visit to the church.

That photo-op was beyond shocking, pathetic, and clouded in contradictions, authoritarianism, and counterfeit deference. Perhaps the most farcical thing Trump has done during his reign—inciting federal officers to "dominate the streets" right before peace was deliberately disrupted with violence on his walk over to the church to hold up a Bible like he was unsure if it was a book or a foam finger. Countless ordinary Americans are displaying acts of immense solidarity and perspective right now, and not a single model of it is emanating from the White House. As we heard a reporter on TV remark, one would have thought he would have gone over to the church to pray. Yeah, right.

Wednesday, June 3rd

There seem to be various non-credible talking heads trying to grapple with the nuances of specific weapons used by the Park Police and the purpose of Trump's photo-op. If one still remains skeptical after giving this a modicum of thought, then caring about this clarification is categorically indicative of being against the cause.

When my friends and I arrived on Monday evening there was nothing violent to be seen, only a peaceful demonstration (albeit in a fulminating manner) and a wall of officers on the Lafayette lawn. All of that ceased before the curfew hit. Rubber bullets and stun grenades are confirmed, and that's when the crowd retreated. There was a substantial amount of smoke in the air, and everyone on the ground with us was screaming "tear gas". I wasn't affected but my friends said they could feel slight agitation in their eyes. The Mayor of D.C. has condemned the tear gas use, thereby validating the reality of the situation, but (as stated previously) there are several outlets saying that it was not used but rather smoke bombs and pepper balls instead. Regardless, as one Twitter observer noted, "a gaseous, tear-inducing mixture" was used with an identical molecular appearance and had the exact same effect on innocent citizens (as seen on videos on the streets of that same day of people washing their eyes out with milk and water). There is substantial documentation that mace was definitely used yesterday, and sting ball grenades were left in the street. Plus, to sum it up, the definition of tear gas by the CDC explicitly includes pepper spray gas so there's not really any valuable distinction there. Obviously, every component matters but this one still seems unambiguously worthy of condemnation. These false claims that are being peddled around by ignorant bodies sum up the aim of this entire administration of the past four years: To warp reality to fit a lying narrative, even in the face of living through the truth.

Another comparison floating around has been to recall moments in history reminiscent of the current period of unrest. This has not been the first time that the national guard has gassed peaceful protesters, is one sample of these comments. Another is that black Americans have enjoyed economic and social improvements in their standards of living in the past 50 years. The relevance here is tremendously dubious. It minimizes the experience of those who have been hurt by it in the present. Some of these touted remarks are simply not useful, and this is primarily expressed based on circumstance. This takes the appearance of a symptom of the evolution of how recent generations have consumed history. Classifications of the former comparison have been named by Nietzsche, who wrote that one can make exclamations that showcase a "knowledge of culture", or of history, rather than invoking a creative or functional use of that knowledge. A reflection on how this moment in time is a mirror to the past seems to be mere declarations of information and attempts to sloganize history.

Friday, June 5th

My roommate and I went to D.C. again on Wednesday night with thousands of others. We marched to the Capitol, which as of late can sometimes take on the appearance of being shrouded in even more corruption than the White House. As we reached Constitution Avenue, the picture to our left would provide an imposing realization. Etched on the building that used to house the Newseum, on a plaque the size of the building itself, were the inscribed words of the first amendment. We were actively playing out the personification of an idea—one of the most crucial freedoms of our country as it hung in the sky. One that had been infringed upon just days ago:

"Congress shall make no law respecting an establishment of religion, or prohibiting the free exercise thereof; or abridging the freedom of speech, or of the press; or the right of the people peaceably to assemble, and to petition the Government for a redress of grievances."

Upon our return to McPherson Square, our horde experienced the next 8 minutes and 46 seconds as a collective. We laid on our backs. The timer started. For those next few minutes, I drifted in and out of lucid thought. Sometimes I could hear and even softly participated in the mob yelling "I can't breathe", sometimes I could only hear my own voice, and sometimes I felt like I could hear nothing at all. My eyes were locked on the sky. A plane flew by from the right. I thought about the flight of souls and the vastness of the space that is suspended above us each waking moment. Eventually, the living take their place in that void, leaving their ghosts behind along with the choice on how to respond to their absence. Rarely are we all allowed to share an emotion, much less an asseveration that will be sketched along the scroll of history. To participate in such an occasion was a product of my own luck and privilege. It was an honor to redeem the memory of George Floyd for a flicker of time on earth; time which he should have been able to share with us.

That very night, our favorite band canceled a virtual "Living Room Concert" they had scheduled for Friday: *"The gravity of this moment in history calls for complete attention,"* they wrote. The mindfulness of that gesture cannot be overstated.

Tuesday, June 9th

There's a certain rhythm when things come in the form of the number three—from the first book of Caesar, Kant's three critiques, to the very divisions and segments of existence (birth, life, and death). It seems to have a mystical significance that cannot be fully grasped. So, as it happens, I would like to address three notions that have surfaced in response to the Black Lives Matter movement that I deem to be in maximal bad taste, and conclude with an explanation that carries the same pulse of the number, and hopefully will serve to provide an understanding and utility for the means of political comprehension.

The first of these responses may seem rather innocuous and even intuitive. Many have asserted that cops deserve the presumption of innocence as well, especially since "not all cops are bad," which is a tautology as argumentatively significant as "skyscrapers are tall". Is anyone saying the opposite? "Not all cops are bad" does not follow any claim that is currently being seriously discussed. A systemic problem does not mean that every moving cog in the machine is corrupt. But the perplexing element is the reflex to defend cops. Surely, we need to be defending the victims rather than the aggressors. Both can be done given that they are not mutually exclusive, but the matter of prioritization is of interest. In other words, the presumption of innocence for cops is not the main subject on the national stage. It is how they are members of a fractured institution that is guilty of racist attitudes and excessive force which has been a main contributor to the historical black experience in America. Instead of these empty assertions about the behavior of cops, immediate sympathy should take precedent. Black lives matter. The black experience in America is unquestionably different than any other group in our nation's history, and nobody should have to explain why, or seriously question the vitriol from their communities and families. The defense of police officers comes at the last hour of the day, after we have taken ample time during the morning, afternoon, and night to address the vexation from the black community.

"If George Floyd had been white, he would be with us today" has drawn serious objections. The outrage as a result of this sentence has been quite odd. Why so defensive? To defend the unknown intentions of Chauvin is a symptom of a magnifying glass that needs to zoom out. This murder will be dealt with on the individual level within the means of the law, but our responsibility as a nation is to discuss this problem not at the level of the individual, but rather a system. The pervasive and historic problem at hand is within police departments across the country and the systemic racist behavior. All of this needs to be dealt with in the context of history, as well. The reason the former claim works, and is useful in my opinion, is because it's not confined within literal parameters. It is a counter-factual, and therefore logically impossible to "prove", but these are useful in arguments to illustrate something beyond direct epistemological certainties. To quickly invoke a technical subtlety, the sentence is a "bearer of truth" in its proposition due to the accumulated evidence at our disposal that lends credence to police brutality, the skewed and disproportionate injuries and killings of black men and women, and how the police have escaped all of this with relative impunity. It's an assertion about corruption within a broken system perpetuated by those who are supposed to protect every human regardless of their race. And for people to deny and hiss at this is indicative of uncertainty surrounding the blatant history of legal oppression and injustice. Tragically, sometimes it really is solely about race and not about all of these fatuous nuances, including the one that we cannot know for sure whether Chauvin was racist.

Lastly is the issue of violent protests—the seemingly sole infatuation of the media. To begin, the instances of violence are a speck of dust compared to the number of citizens who have used their voice to protest and nothing else. Claims for

BLM to disassociate itself from the extremist acts on the street are correct, and this has been done, but mindful observers will note that this distinction should be automatic. Any inclination otherwise is to signify being at the will of the news sources and their chosen coverage. The question as to why black men and women have resorted to violence in the wake of this movement is epically important, and I earnestly hope everyone has spent time wondering themselves. Violence in it of itself is morally reprehensible. But there are instances in which society permits violence. Such a point is up for debate for the civil rights movement in the sixties, and the question becomes whether this has the capacity to join the same classification.

Now more than ever is a proper time to re-visit Martin Luther King's "I Have a Dream" speech. He states that the black community has been given a bad check by America, and for a paragraph artfully writes of the theft of prosperity and unalienable rights contained within the promissory note. The chosen economic theme was no accident as it echoes both Frederick Douglass and W.E.B. DuBois. As is the case with most well-known pieces of oratory, there are several phrases that do not get the historical attention they deserve from being upstaged by other memorable uses of rhetoric. There is no special literary draw to the phrase that caught my eye upon a second glance at the speech, and it can even be read with an exasperated breath of a veracious ultimatum rather than an inspirational call to action. King simply states that if America is to be a great nation, the dream he speaks of must come true.

There is no counter, there is no follow-up, there is no alternative. If America is to be a great nation, it has to represent the best means of democratic order in the world. The very fact that the country erupted in such anger after George Floyd should be a hint that something is clearly lopsided. There is much to do to ensure that generations ahead are treated not by the color of their skin, but by the content of their character. Part of this vision is a future where the oppressed do not have to resort to violence because there will be no instigation. Let us not forget that the genesis of the movement was spawned from a violent act of murder. Omitting this rather vital tidbit makes the rebuttal seem a bit sinister. Nobody should want to be held occupying the position that, sure, men and women are victims of brutal homicides but that does not mean justice has to be in the form of violence. This is incomplete—the crimes themselves must be put to an end so there is no chance of a retaliatory strike. Only then will we be able to act as a beacon to the rest of the world, when America can truly meet "physical force with soul force" as King declares. Violence is an unquestionable part of world history, and certainly American history. To acknowledge anything otherwise would be woefully ignorant. Although history isn't written on the street, that is certainly where it begins.

In common law, there is a principle called the "duty to retreat". It states that one must fully exhaust all possible escape routes before violence is imposed on the attacker. The United States has dispensed with this legal requirement and substituted this notion for "stand your ground" laws instead. An Indiana court once wrote that "the tendency of the American mind seems to be very strongly against" a duty to retreat, which, as a reason for a ruling, is satirical at best and just idiotic at worst. It should be no surprise that homicide rates rise by 7% in states where stand your ground laws are passed. A handful of states have even adopted "castle doctrines" which say that persons threatened at home have the right to use "reasonable force, including deadly force, to defend their property, person, or another." All in all, the lever of the law does protect people who use violence as a means to protect themselves when threatened, and the very same people who oppose the violent protests would surely find shelter under this law if they themselves were threatened. (I would also be interested in a headcount of those on the other side and their support of the death penalty) Is it so hard to digest this idea when ballooned up from the individual level?

For one thing, the destruction of property and businesses that have had nothing to do with the maltreatment of anyone is disgraceful and hard to see. On an individual level, there is no excuse for the demolition of commerce and looting. But, to purposefully belabor the point, this must be viewed from a different vantage point that requires an impressive amount of empathy. How would it feel to see that the only people throughout history who were owned, lynched in front of public audiences, hunted down for crimes the law acquitted them for, powerless to vote and enact change, and treated by the police as scum and animals, had *your* skin color? White America does not have a clue. Institutions have dominion over us, at least more than people do, and those who enforce the law account for one of the most crucial pillars of our society. They are guardians, protectors of order. What are we to do when those who protect us no longer do? How is the black community to respond when they have attempted peace in the past, only to see no changes in the status quo? *Who watches the watchers?* If you do not find it more egregious that armed officers of the state have attacked empty-handed citizens than the paltry crimes that occur even outside times of political unrest, I greatly urge you to reconsider. Cops are indicted for *less than 1% of killings*, while citizens are prosecuted at a rate of 90%. Perhaps we are seeing that a populace is only as good as those who govern them.

Every day of consuming the news and responses to this conversation, there has been one explanation that cuts through all tribal coalitions of thought. As promised, the theory that I have continuously found serviceable to understand the rousing and reasoning of this carnival of political commentary comes from Arnold Kling, with the following insight on the three languages of politics: The right talks in terms of "civilization" and "barbarism", the left talks in terms of the "oppressor" and the "oppressed", and libertarians talk in terms of "freedom" and "coercion". The former value vectors are responsible, nearly across the board, for how individuals strung across the political spectrum digest and regurgitate what they believe to be the most prevalent matters at hand in the arena of politics.

Sunday, June 14th

During the DNC in Chicago of 1968, protests rang out in the streets to a very similar sound that can be heard around the nation today. The startling contemporary resemblance was such that it brought to my attention the grounds to uncouple any personal motives for supporting the Black Lives Matter movement from the overall response of the country. I suspect there is a gap within everyone who has participated in protests between their personal motivations and the public branding of the events. The same problem exists now as it did in Chicago: sometimes the social perception of these functions has been different from the actual voices on the street.

The minutiae of the protests *will* be important, no doubt, but the broader historic implication will side with the movement as being reasonable opposed to unreasonable. A full 30 years removed from the generation and outbursts of 1968, Peter Robinson sat down with Christopher Hitchens and William F. Buckley to discuss the same matters of self-indulgence, naiveté, and sophisticated ideology among the sixties left in their opprobrium to an unjust and imperialist war in Vietnam. Hitchens recalled a slogan painted on the walls of Paris which read: "Take your desires for reality", which can now be thought of as yet another quotation that, I believe, members of the right would like to attach to the fight against legal racism as an instance of hedonism and opportunism. This is a shallow desire on both ends if proven to be true, but does not immolate the sentiment that has been a festering sore on the country even after the civil rights movement.

Regrettably, it would be grandiose to assert that this time around leaves us with a much clearer vision on where to stand. If Buckley were still with us he would probably echo his formulation that he held about the civil rights movement and apply it to the current circumstances, which was none other than a look of disdain on the disorder, regarding it as anti-thought and anti-rational. Buckley, to his credit, eventually saw the benefit to the Civil Rights Movement. At the time, he was quick to say that the programs to advance the black cause were a "formulaic response" to a real problem. It was only later that he granted that they achieved more than some other means of constitutional decorum might have done.

'68 saw protesters who had purposefully burned their draft cards to avoid being shipped over to a country they could not even locate on a map, while other young men followed the questionable instructions from the government and were used as pawns in a war that is now seen, as Hitchens puts it, as "much more as a crime than a mistake or blunder". The BLM protests have been seen not just across all 50 states, but across the world, and the overwhelming majority have been conducted with grace and poise. It is inevitable that with a movement as large as this one, that there are times of departure from the very reasonable requests of the black community. Does this in any way diminish the takeaway? We should be doing everything to ensure the next 50 years are not subject to the same oppression as the last.

I have always thought that the order of the world seems the most balanced when effects from injustices have (at least) proportional responses to their causes. In other words, the longer George Floyd had a knee to his throat, the louder the uproar. This movement is a noble part of American history, and when future generations ask us why it took so long to establish equal rights they will be met with replies about the entrenched blowback of the original sin of this country. The scars of slavery will always be with us, but it is our responsibility to live with the knowledge of them without letting them be seen.

DESPAIR ON THE NATURE OF THINGS

Converting dejection to ambition

Optimism bears a charm rarely challenged, and is the precise shadow casting over the lens of reality. Hope has an ingratiating way about it, especially as one attempts to make sense of the suffering around the globe. Imperfections seem ubiquitous upon an honest look at world events. They come on a spectrum of intensity, but only in two forms: problems with which we have the agency to change, and those we can't budge. There is a jumbled mismatch concerning our volition to enact change to the issues at hand. As more of us take comfort underneath this blanket of optimism, there's a receding incentive to act accordingly to bring balance to what is evidently array.

All of us rest under a numeric value to label us as change agents, according to Cass Sunstein. For example, somebody who is a "0" has no problem reacting to any form of injustice immediately upon witnessing it for the first time. Individuals who are a "1" or "2" rely on the problem repeating itself before they respond. Once we decide we want to intervene, the subsequent internal calculation turns to the opportunity cost of intervening. Sometimes, it is simply not worth the sacrifice of time and energy. Other times the situation might very well constitute action in a conceptual sense, but the problem itself is out of our control. There's no need to stand up from your couch from an impending nuclear attack, for instance. Very seldom does everything align: a mutable problem, a willing change agent, and the means to act. All of this considered, the outcome of where and when we choose to spend our energy still arrives at the depressing conclusion that our decision rationality is askew.

Planet earth and humanity create a living entity that is ceaselessly monitored and observed by its inhabitants. It is split between events enabled by our primate species and the natural effects of our ecosystem. And each person, whether consciously or unconsciously, has an outlook on the natural state of the world that balances both former components into the assessment. The health of the world lies on a spectrum that weighs all of the justice, happiness, and prosperity against all of the suffering, calamities, and injustice. The former end of the continuum represents achievable human perfection and the other constitutes absolute hell. Currently, it is impossible to ignore the following: suffering abounds while prosperity scatters.

The disparity of the nature of order contributes to this greatly, for the ease of inviting disruption outweighs the labor for restoring it all. The level of effort in starting a house fire, for example, vastly outweighs the work to restore the disastrous outcome. Chaos is easy, while order is arduous. One might argue that the current state of the world is in the best condition in the history of the universe. Incredible technology and vast innovation in science and medicine have allowed mankind to flourish with what would have been illusory ease at any point in the past. But the problems have merely evolved and are therefore different. Instead of attempting to avoid death by bacteria in our teeth at age 23, we now are dealing with the future effects of climate change.

Optimists look at the previous spectrum and see a positive future, but viewing the world in a state of relative good standing consequently acts as a bulwark against personal surges of action to restore the balance of liberty, justice, and good around the globe. Pragmatists, realists, and even cynics are essential personas to point to the unsettling actuality of existing in the twenty first century.

Many of the epic problems of our time are out of the hands of many individuals: foreign government interference in elections, pandemics and epidemics, impunity in Mexico, fraud and conspiracy in Brazil, war in the Middle East, a timeless divide in Northern Ireland over the same religion, malnourished and disease-ridden neighborhoods in Africa, economic crises hanging in suspense, purposeful swindling of financial markets, active sex trafficking in Asia, Iran, Israel, and the United States, mountainous glaciers breaking off in Antarctica, opioid deaths skyrocketing, and the slow evaporation of the love for knowledge. For these, most individuals rely on the autonomy to elect representatives who will hopefully address these issues with the best solutions. It appears the best we can do (although the effective altruism movement is slowly disproving this) and will remain an important function.

Meanwhile, the rest of us can be focused on things within our control. We can respond the first time, rather than the second, third, or fourth. Often this is easier than it may seem, but it comes with an honest look at the world around us and the exigent need for everyone to suit up. And even if your capacity to improve on the nature of things is limited, or even negligible, acknowledging that mankind is in a losing struggle is still progress of a kind. Sam Harris puts it distinctly: *"Changing how you respond to the world is often as good as changing it."* Optimism is admirable in certain contexts, but history is an arbiter that has sided with those who have fought against the status quo. There is always work to be done and it begins from a place of discontentment.

The work to rebuild prosperity much exceeds the work to destroy it. Anybody who is partial to the Nietzschian idea of all good things must originate from bad things will acknowledge that the framework of deriving motivation from disarray as a suitable system to identify compassion, and hopefully subsequent action, in the world. Without an impetus to improve upon the nature of things, mankind will relinquish any possession of autonomy and fall victim to the bystander effect, always assuming that another problem will be solved by a third party. As optimism casts its shadow over the true order of the world, remaining content with the comfort it offers would simply be a grave mistake.

ON FREE WILL

Are we puppets or authors?

FATE, LUCK, PROVIDENCE, CHOICE, DESTINY, CHANCE — THESE words comprise much of how we communicate about the nature of our past, present, and future. Each have their respective meanings, but they all encompass a concept that is fundamental to understanding our agency as humans: free will. Since passion is invoked more rigorously in threats that remove autonomy rather than grant it, a significant number of people feel that life would lose all meaning if free will did not exist or was a myth. The very nature of the human condition invites us all to want to be the conscious arbiter of our actions and choices. In the words of William Ernest Henley, we desire to be the masters of our fate and the captains of our souls. An introductory pamphlet to free will can assist to see if Henley's sentiment can be played out.

The most fascinating dichotomy in intellectual conundrums is that between how the world actually is, and what we wish it to be. We all *feel* and hopefully *want* to be free, but there are several barricades to square these two desires. Knowledge derived from observations and experience, formally referred to as *a posteriori* reasoning, provides an incomplete picture of consciousness. Wishful thinking crowds out additional critical faculties. The problem of free will attacks the deepest intuitions about life itself and requires the aid of multiple disciplines to arrive at the truth. Imagine a storyteller narrating the events on earth. How would our actions be described? The Stoics suggested a dismal narrative with their depressing metaphor about the stage we all share. We are each assigned a role to play in the tragedy of life, they proposed, and there is no room for improvisation between the prescribed lines each of us see on our scripts. Unpalatable at first, to turn away from the idea in a flash of displeasure is certainly justifiable. Such detractors will then find the other possibility much more appealing. The world is, instead, a place of infinite freedom and choice, with no outside forces acting upon the decisions of the players. Or is it somehow a combination of both? And there you have it. We are either completely free, not free at all, or somewhere on the spectrum.

Dialogues currently exist on the modern and historical literature on free will with the purpose to connect the conclusions with everyday banter about human volition, but they are complex and jargon-filled discussions usually with no ending. The objective should be to arrive at an understanding where the puzzle pieces of experience, reality, consequence, and language can interlock. This is where phrases such as "If it is meant to be, it will be", or "Everything happens for a reason" and others said in regard to responsibility of an action require cross-examination and start to crumble. It is in our best interest to ensure that the realities of free will and common language governing our discourse live in tandem with one another and are not constantly flouted. Further comprehension of this relationship can lead to a deeper understanding of the will and intent of our fellow primates. The mass murderer Charles Whitman was not acting of his own choosing on that fateful day in Texas, for instance, but was at the mercy of a large brain tumor pressing intently on his amygdala. Hate, blame, and motive are all called to the witness stand upon further investigation into the extent of *how much we actually control* about our lives. Living an examined life requires a refinement of these clashing issues and is the doorway to the most equitable criminal justice system to adjudicate problems like the one above.

Let's say you have the option of wearing either a blue hat or yellow hat this morning. The starting position for this choice assumes that all human beings have entirely free actions. This claim is the essence of libertarianism (different than the political ideology), the most flexible of options. The metaphysical concept of cause and effect, something we hold to be as inescapable as gravity, is at the crux of all free will conundrums. Effects are parsed into two categories: event causality and agent causality. A physical event such as a bowling ball rolling down its lane has to have a physical cause, for instance, and cannot independently begin its trajectory toward the pins. Many libertarians concede this and reach no further. To demur against event causality would be equivalent to the temporary suspension of Newtonian physics. Agent causality is different because it involves internal thoughts and decisions and is the altar for the libertarian ideas. Your decision to choose one hat over the other *independent of any and all external factors* would lend credence to this causal structure. You just "decided" to wear the blue hat. The libertarian sense excludes any mention of whether your favorite color is blue, if it was a new or old hat, or any other contextual factor. The notion that an agent "could have done otherwise" has been the untouchable island of agreement in philosophy to define the autonomy of an agent. The origin of this decision is somewhat inexplicable by libertarians. It certainly *feels* like a free decision, but the final answer was either randomly generated in your brain, or, was there all along. So, could you *really* have chosen the yellow hat? Determinism says you could not.

Your decision was influenced by a plethora of factors, a determinist would argue, and you could not have chosen differently from what you were already determined to do. Libertarianism has lately become rather untenable and quickly refuted by the realities of determinism, which holds an opposite thesis — all human decisions are already determined by external forces, and can be predicted if access to the culmination of influencing factors were known. These factors include everything from chemical reactions in our neural networks to the time in history in which we were born. Before launching the analysis of why this may very well be the case, the dismal connotation requires an address. This deterministic viewpoint need not imply a fatalist mindset. Fatalism concludes that the future of all events on earth are already planned *independent* of human thought or action. The future is not inevitable in a deterministic world but would be in a fatalistic one. Luckily, the fatalistic view holds no logical basis in reality. "Inevitable", rightfully defined by Daniel Dennett, really means "unavoidable". And being able to avoid an event, such as an incoming brick, is a desirable power in the proverbial arsenal of free will. (But as Dennett asks: *was it ever really going to hit you?*) If fate has it that an intruder will enter and burglarize your house, it is futile to put a lock on your door. The burglar will enter your house anyway. Unlike determinism, fatalism is independent of causality and is an ontological wasteland. The intruder will succeed regardless of any Herculean retaliation from you, and the brick will connect with your skull even if you see it coming, because all of those actions are preordained as well.

A deterministic reality can rightfully lead to a defeatist mindset as well, even with events that are supposedly joyful. If you are destined to marry a particular person, is life itself intrinsically ludicrous? While some people are fated to end up with supermodels, others are destined to remain alone. Here is where we find the concept of *destiny* levied into the debate. The invocation of a supernatural architect is where mayhem begins, which is why many philosophers elect to leave the proposition out of their case. Theological justifications for free will are scattered across the map and invoke different definitions for personal liberty at every step. An immediate example would be the Dutch book of a world view in which an intervening God has a plan for all humanity, and for the life of the espouser in particular, but a simultaneous belief that mankind is endowed with unlimited free will. Since claims about the omnipotence of God and the scalability of his power are questions that are not falsifiable, any insertion of a supernatural being should be compatible with any thought about free will, including fatalism. It just depends on nuanced assumptions about things God has or has not set in motion. This can only be partially justified with a presupposition about the theological framework of the universe since, in this example, God has chosen where we are free and where we are not. An explanation for a belief in free will and a deity is possible but must be couched in the recognition that there are unconfirmed theological assumptions embedded in any and all claims.

Determinism says that every choice we *appear* to consciously author is no more than the product of past experiences and characteristics that were not under our control. Our lives, bodies, and minds operate as systems, with countless external inputs. The entirety of these catalysts for our actions can never be fully realized, but determinists say it would provide everything we need to know about how an agent will act.

Neuroscience studies are attempting to make this an emergent truth, but have yet to seduce the academic community with their fMRI analyses to advocate on their vital contributions. Unsurprisingly, humans are exceedingly susceptible to invisible tricks played on the mind. Daniel Kahneman, the winner of the Nobel Prize in Economics in 2002, has found many examples of how easily they can occur. He discusses a study in his prize lecture that asked college students how happy they were with their life and to identify how many dates they had been on in the past month. Given in the aforementioned order, the correlation was negligible. When reversed, it rose to 0.66. If there is one thing we *should be* in tune with more than anything, it is our balance of happiness and suffering, but the mere order of questions caused answers to fluctuate. This is a judgement heuristic that plays on our immediate emotions. Examples of the unconscious manipulation of our brains are seemingly ubiquitous nowadays and they are imperative to understanding our (perceived) agency.

Sometimes our cognitive influences are not innocuous, but devilishly contrived. Manipulation by the purposeful alteration of reality is an additional testament to a deterministic universe. Perhaps the utmost example of this can be found in the work of Derren Brown, the illusionist. A few years ago he engineered a social experiment called *The Push* to see how far an ordinary person could be convinced to commit appalling acts. He staged an environment filled with actors with the exception of one individual—his subject. The results were akin to the Stanford Prison experiment, and reveal the influential extent of our surroundings.

At the very least, we can grant that determinism covers a large portion of our lives. The remaining questions are the following: In which domains of life, if any, are we still uninhibited and free? Is it the type of free will we want? And lastly, is it the type of free will that matches *how it feels* to be free? These questions all create the final space for our personal liberty, our "elbow room" for free will as Daniel Dennett calls it, and the associated implications of accountability and meaning that come from the answers.

Compatibilism is the third variety of free will belief. Compatibilists station themselves at the gates of sovereignty and freedom. They grant our ability to make choices and argue that a deterministic world and free will are, in fact, compatible. The compatibilist defense of free will can best be demonstrated by peeling back the layers of hard determinism through a thought experiment developed and popularized by Sam Harris: Think of a city. It can be any city in the world. Commit just one to memory before reading the next sentence. To begin, there are several (at least) cities in the world that you could not possibly have named because you do not know that they exist. (Ngerulmud, for instance, is a city that I did not know existed until a moment ago when I randomly googled for it.) There are, as Sam points out, many cities that we all know but did not appear in our heads as viable options for the question. Baghdad, for instance, could be a city that you know of but did not occur to you while your brain was combing through cities. So, consider this: Were you free to choose *that which did not occur to you to choose?* If you only thought of London, Chicago, and Kyoto, were you free to choose Baghdad? Thoughts do seem to simply arise in the mind, and we are unable to influence which ones do and do not. Mozart even represented this when articulating the origin of his musical ideas: "Whence and how do they come? I do not know and I have *nothing to do with it*".

Harris carves out his definition of free will such that this is a problem. Referencing our thoughts, he says the fact that we don't "think them before we think them" is an attack on our perception of our free will. But this seems relatively harmless. If our minds operated as such, we would have quite the landscape of thoughts at our disposal before we select the ones we choose to become our own. The fact that thoughts are different based on experience and one's information diet is justifiable, not objectionable.

Charles Renouvier, a French philosopher, views the spontaneous arrival of thoughts and ideas as inevitable but the subsequent leap in action as a vital characteristic of what it means to be free. The thoughts themselves may appear in flashes with inexplicable origins, but *our choice to continue thinking* about one or the other, and to further examine it, is another matter altogether. There are many other facets of this problem in which second-order derivations of ontology and metaphysics are acceptable within a compatibilist position.

Many of the same dilemmas revolve around the idea of choice. Compatibilists say that an action can be deemed free (more or less) if the consideration for the ultimate end is an internal examination. The main problem, due to advanced science, is that the line of internal versus external contributors is quite often blurred. The idea of what it *feels like* to be free seems to be fundamental in this sense. In terms of appearance, the option to choose one hat over another can be cognitively no different from determining to rob a bank. The principle of alternate possibilities suggests that one can only be held accountable for either action if he or she was able to refrain from the action ultimately chosen. By acting as conscious agents with the ability to change results for the future benefit of oneself or someone else, probable ends can be shifted a degree left or right, which can mean everything and make all the difference. Compatibilism, in many more strains than determinism, offers compelling reasons to always behave that someone can be reasoned with or persuaded by an outside source, or by themselves. By this reasoning, acting as if one has complete control over all actions is an entirely sensible way forward, but only if carried out in knowledge of the fact that there are always multiple puppet strings active behind the scenes.

Free will is ominous. A lot has yet to be resolved and the meaning of freedom in the context of consciousness has unquestionably changed over the course of history. Part of this mystery is an illusion, but not fully. The true identity of our agency matters a great deal in a multitude of settings.

If nothing else, the alignment between what our minds have us *believe* about the nature of our thoughts and actions compared to the real influences behind all we think and execute is of paramount importance. By augmenting our awareness of these details, the world can only make more sense, not less.

MODERN PROPHECIES

Rampant obedience to the act of predicting

PROPHETS USED TO ENJOY SOLITUDE PREDOMINANTLY IN religious texts and stories. They served as the mouthpiece of a deity and were worshiped for their inexplicable celestial announcements. In the Bible, some of these proclamations came from deities themselves. Before the cock crowed, as it says in the book of Matthew, Jesus prophesied his disciple David would deny him three times. Beginning as servants for the messages of the supernatural, the twenty-first century has seen the role of the prophet move from those who were "chosen" to presumably anybody with functioning vocal cords. Predictions on all sorts of matters, mundane to crucial, fill the airwaves of conversation with an appearance hard to detect. While feasibly innocuous by nature, there is a foul property to them perfectly coinciding with the already prevalent degradation of truth and — perhaps of equal importance — trust.

Nowhere is this symptom more apparent than in the staggering number of estimates on the magical date of departure of the coronavirus from non-epidemiologists, doctors, or medical professionals of any kind. (As if this pandemic can be solved outside the science laboratory.) These frictionless proclamations come from a shameless band of dolts. Bearing the same clothing of divinity, these clerics in holy orders and fortune tellers have been banishing the deadly virus from the earth for months on end to no avail. It is nothing more or less than astounding that avid listeners of this enlightened ensemble can claim to know how the pandemic will unfold when no seer predicted its arrival. The same spurious confidence spills over into many other territories, and luckily are benign compared to the recklessness of touting baseless beliefs on a public health crisis.

Another common occurrence usually tries to invite a sense of bewilderment from names from the past. Isaac Asimov, the headline will read, predicted the current state of technological advancement in education. Or other assertions by famous historical figures will be used in a Hail Mary attempt to will a concept into existence. Benjamin Franklin's wish that the human body may be preserved after death and eventually revived is somehow used to prop up the inevitability that one day this may occur and, as Franklin desired for himself, mortals will be preserved in a vat of madeira wine. Meanwhile, other headlines read that the end of meat will arrive in twenty years and conquering Mars will be seen on television in a few generations. All of this does nothing to advance ideas forward, much less defend notions of the future.

Predictions flood the corporate sector as well as mainstream media. Alex Murrell at Epoch Design investigated websites of three major consulting firms for forecasts on any subject matter for the years 2025 to 2050. The results ranged from 3,000 to nearly 7,000 predictions per site. Not included are the projections these businesses also make for the next *one hundred years and beyond.* "We're still finding our feet in this century" he writes, "but some, it seems, already understand the next." Nowadays the public sphere seems to be filled with this level of volume. It is driven by a misleading impression. Predictions are easy placeholders for knowledge. A conjecture that turns out to be true offers a high payoff but costs very little, if anything at all. It is assumed that to proffer a prediction must mean an understanding of the matter at hand, which is seldom the case. Forecasts of all kinds become more important if spread by people in power, so it will always be prudent to ensure any such prognosis was researched thoroughly. Society needs to alleviate itself of this attitude of mind: quick to predict and yet impossible to change. A conception of the probability of the future necessarily changes behavior of the present. Expectations are a powerful tool and not to be carelessly littered during serious conversations and endeavors.

Many fields in academia are the (relatively) nascent apprentices to Kierkegaard's famous line, *"Life can only be understood backwards; but it must be lived forwards"*. Predictive methodologies in the social sciences, in particular, seem devoted to developing mathematical ways of forecasting what is statistically likely to happen based on what *has happened* in the past, or from what is *currently happening* in the present. These are all worthy pursuits, but these types of predictions should be viewed with an advisable eye and never as certainties. However, esoteric corners of academia should still be reserved for lofty but potentially unexpected discoveries. For instance, if we could predict war, could we *prevent* it? The effort sounds as Herculean as it is, but was the precise objective of the English mathematician Lewis Fry Richardson. He first hypothesized that the rate of increase in armaments of a country was proportional to that of an adversary nation, as well as the grievances felt toward that nation. A second theory followed, which postulated that the propensity of war between two countries is a function of their shared border length. It was while studying the border lengths of countries in which he discovered the fractal nature of their shape, which by happenstance has been more of a contribution to mathematics and theoretical physics than his war theory on geopolitics. Breakthroughs have no roadmap. The research dome must always hold enough space for the next project to understand more of the universe.

It is always the mundane that surprises when tangled with something of great importance. It's the great seduction of the riddle — the overlooked piece of the question at hand, as in the end of *To Kill a Mockingbird*, when Tom Robinson's innocence is demonstrated by the simple fact that he is *left*-handed. Every once in a while, outcomes on election day will be affected simply because it rained, an example of which offers the essence of the notion of the future. Simple explanations for why certain events unfold and others do not are more palatable than the complicated ones. This can happen sporadically but never consistently. But adhering to this would be to go against what Stephen Hawking said in his millennium interview. "I think the next century," he uttered, *"will be the century of complexity."* Annoyed with the precariousness of the future, it is easier to want to believe others have it figured out. Yet this does not mean to accept predictions on a whim. Civilization has come a long way since the era of prophecies and prophets. Chaos theory suggests infinitesimal changes from a given state of affairs can have enormous effects, and therefore should render unpredictability as a fixed cost. In a world with the largest information reservoir in history, a great downfall awaits for the populace believing it knows more than it can.

COSMIC CONSIDERATIONS

Championing the highest dimension of thought

IT IS EASY TO BE INITIALLY ACCEPTING OF THE VIEWPOINT THAT the world is long past its embryonic stage and mankind has elevated it to an advanced existence. We've built pyramids, explored the ocean, cured polio, and brewed beer. If one were to look for an acknowledgment to swiftly dismiss the previous thought, it can be found quite easily in the upper right-hand corner of a map. North Korea is an enigma, and a callous one at that. Surely a version of a cultivated human race does not contain a theocratic regime of this kind in the picture, one where you can be convicted of thought-crime. The entire topography is one devoid of pleasure and beauty, where citizens are trapped on stretches of land where the birds are bored of flying and the life of a human being is treated as property, and therefore rendered without a purpose. And yet even after conquering space travel and the invention of the internet, although it was not always this way, the unlucky residents of North Korea live in darkness, ignorance, and servility.

Beyond the observance of the 38th parallel, the blue and green marble suspended in the atmosphere provokes even more doubt of anything resembling cosmic adolescence. Earth remains a Type 1 civilization on the Kardashev scale, carrying itself as a dwarf-like planet orbiting quite an ordinary star. And every second outside of the Milky Way, the life span of supporting stars of other galaxies reach their end, solar systems like ours explode and cease to be, taken off the chessboard while our sun continues to burn out its last few billion years before it does the same. The infancy of the only planet known to harbor life is extraordinary, but nothing compared the trivial role in the agenda of the universe. Our temporary lodging is nothing more than a "mote of dust suspended in a sunbeam" as Carl Sagan once said, as he elaborated on the humbling insignificance of our place in the cosmos:

"Our posturings, our imagined self-importance, the delusion that we have some privileged position in the Universe, are challenged by this point of pale light. Our planet is a lonely speck in the great enveloping cosmic dark. In our obscurity, in all this vastness, there is no hint that help will come from elsewhere to save us from ourselves. . .

. . . It has been said that astronomy is a humbling and character-building experience. There is perhaps no better demonstration of the folly of human conceits than this distant image of our tiny world. To me, it underscores our responsibility to deal more kindly with one another, and to preserve and cherish the pale blue dot, the only home we've ever known."

The existence of life elsewhere is a paradox. In the Milky Way alone, there are 1,000,000 potential life-supporting planets similar to our own. We have yet to hear from these civilizations, if they even exist, but the question of their presence arises, especially if Earth is the most advanced society in existence. A potential theory for why there has been so sight of or interaction with any extraterrestrial life has to do with "filters". These represent certain barriers which annihilate all sentient creatures. It is very possible that nuclear war, climate change, or artificial intelligence are the very hurtles that catapult other worlds into their ultimate demise. The explanation is very simply that other advanced life forms have reached these stages and have been defeated by them.

For most of human history, questions were answered on a local basis, at the level of the individual and kin. Problems slowly evolved to a more developed quality as the mind matured and the industrial society deposed the agrarian. No longer was hunting for food a daily chore, and the implementation of the scientific method improved our capacity for discovery. The pressing questions of our time now serve at the national and international dimension — immigration, taxes, welfare, and so forth. Arguments and debates on these matters seldom examine the subject from a cosmic perspective. Perhaps it seems odd to suddenly begin talking about our trajectory towards oblivion on the Senate floor, but there is merit to invoke the perspective from the overall grand scheme of things.

At some point, problems left by the wayside are going to be around the corner. Geoffrey West is a theoretical physicist and the author of *Scale: The Universal Laws of Life, Growth, and Death in Organisms, Cities, and Companies*, a gleaming book of insights. One of his major academic interests has been with cities, and why they never seem to die. Optimization plays a decisive role in all of the biological and ecological schemes discussed in the book, and he stresses how it will also decide the continued existence of the future of humanity. He notes that 15 percent less infrastructure is needed for a city with 10 million people rather than two cities of 5 million people. It is this type of knowledge that must be put to good use if we are to truly augment life on this planet. Scientists are constantly discovering the intricacies of living sustainably. West's enlightening book has an important dialogue on urban development, and outlines the kinds of impacts our civilization will have to take into account when drawing up plans for expansion. He extends beyond urban planning, needless to say, and calls attention to how climate change can affect us at the individual level which, therefore, will have global implications. A two-degree Celsius increase in the global temperature, for instance, would increase the pace of biological life by 20–30% since temperature change is ultimately a chemical reaction with the body. These kinds of linkages increase exponentially to accommodate the oxidative process. Findings such as this one have tremendous effects on resource allocation and usage, growth rates, and mortality rates. Global impacts must be addressed from a consequential basis at the same level, which means leaving the cozy corners of tradition, political pork-barreling, and self-interest.

Civilization can only afford so many catastrophic blunders before all luck runs out. The global poisoning of the DuPont chemical company is one of the more horrific displays the profit motive in recent history. It all began in 1951 when the company began pouring its toxins into local drinking water through digestion ponds. Like a witch at a cauldron, the company concocted a man-made poisonous compound called PFOA (perfluorooctanoic acid) that was a primary ingredient for every Teflon artifact from their factories. Studies were conducted internally which found that working on the Teflon product line was a *literal* death sentence. Their own employees were falling ill and dying at an early age, women were giving birth to children with birth defects, and DuPont did nothing but increase their sales and output. As with the financial crisis in 2007, these sweeping cases never seem to rightfully assign culpability even when the injustices are always disproportionate down the socioeconomic ladder. Just when it would seem self-evident that DuPont would be held responsible, the EPA settlement did not even require them to admit liability. Here is an excerpt from the original journal article outlining the case describing how everyone in the world now has PFOA in their blood:

> "Where scientists have tested for presence of PFOA in the world, they have found it. PFOA is in the blood or vital organs of Atlantic salmon, swordfish, striped mullet, gray seals, common cormorants, Alaskan polar bears, brown pelicans, sea turtles, sea eagles, California sea lions and Laysan albatrosses on Sand Island, a wildlife refuge on Midway Atoll, in the middle of the North Pacific Ocean, about halfway between North America and Asia."

One of these times, the "PFOA" creation of the future will be in a dose too high for the human body to tolerate. Companies, not just individuals, will have to eventually dispense with egocentric attitudes to allow for a flourishing populace and ecosystem. The best replacement for this is undoubtedly the cosmic perspective, a selfless and human-spirited way of looking at all problems.

We live in relation to physical entities and conceptual abstractions, both of which are responsible for how we interact with ideas and the world around us. There is a subtle but robust connection between the two which allows for a refinement of metaphysical interpretations of experience. In stories of great triumph that cement themselves into a book of the extraordinary, there is usually a glimmer of a perennial idea that can be put to good use. That is certainly the case when man first landed on the moon. The observance of Earth from outside its atmosphere and the ability to stare into the never-ending abyss demonstrates that the higher one can physically view the world, the more one can understand it. From the cosmic perspective, astronauts write of an overwhelming shared connectedness. Ignoring it is not an option. Peering back at the pale blue dot that harbors what could be the only life in the universe is something only few have witnessed with their own eyes, but the impacts equip the rest of us with the idea itself. With the oneness of our place in the cosmos comes a soul-stirring reflection, and yet again, one that is impossible to ignore:

> "We are going to die, and that makes us the lucky ones. Most people are never going to die because they are never going to be born. The potential people who could have been here in my place but who will in fact never see the light of day outnumber the sand grains of the Sahara. Certainly those unborn ghosts include greater poets than Keats, scientists greater than Newton. We know this because the set of possible people allowed by our DNA so massively exceeds the set of actual people. In the teeth of these stupefying odds it is you and I, in our ordinariness, that are here. We privileged few, who won the lottery of birth against all odds, how dare we whine at our inevitable return to that prior state from which the vast majority have never stirred."
>
> —*Richard Dawkins*

Dawkins reminds us that we are merely lucky bursts of stardust, given a few privileged breaths before retreating back into nothingness. Each of us is a character introduced for a brief amount of time to deliver a soliloquy to add to the story of the universe. Let it not be forgotten that it is noble to live in honor of those who will never have a chance, and that all of this is worthy of consideration for problems of all sizes, because even those will one day vanish.

THE PLAGUE

On Camus and the absurd

THE TOWN OF ORAN IS A FRENCH PORT SITTING ON THE Algerian coast and is the singular setting for the story of a resurgence of *la peste* written by Albert Camus in 1947. A line from Ginsberg describes the feel of the book; the reader encounters "...*the impulse of winter midnight streetlight small town rain...*" with the sound of a weeping violin coming from the alleys, a fog of dread, and ominous clouds hovering above the guiltless buildings and restaurants. A silent chill accompanies the turning of pages, yet it is somehow reassuring rather than alarming. Very early it is known that the reader is in the hands of brilliance. The characters are methodically placed and masterfully invented. Camus writes with a mindful awareness of the human condition, and his cunning perception runs throughout but begins as such:

> *"Perhaps the easiest way of making a town's acquaintance is to ascertain how the people in it work, how they love, and how they die. In our little town, all three are done on much the same lines, with the same feverish yet casual air. The truth is that everyone is bored, and devotes himself to cultivating habits."*

There is not a word out of place in Camus' masterpiece. It is one part of his acclaimed literary pyramid, responsible for elevating him to receive the Nobel Prize in Literature, alongside *The Stranger* (1942) and *The Fall* (1956). Public attention has turned to *The Plague* given the timely nature of the world's own pandemic, and within the pages one will thankfully not find cliché of the moment, platitudes, or banality, but rather a timeless portrayal of themes encountered across every age, all of which comprise the ravel of mortality in the midst of life. Before long, the reader is met with an acknowledgment, a confession to themselves: the desolate air attached to the thought of death is draped around every construct to life, not simply the apparent ones, and ignoring it is one of the most evolved tricks of modernity.

Of Time

Fleeting existence can lower the spirit if you allow it. We live moment to moment, entranced by the present and captivated by our striving. Suddenly those moments evaporate, the grasp on time is loosened despite the desire to shatter the gears to the clock. Schopenhauer captured this in his essay, *On the Vanity of Existence*, when he ghostly penned, "Time is that by virtue of which everything becomes nothingness in our hands and loses all real value." Although this notion is the essence of how consciousness operates with reality, and has an unforgiving nihilistic flavor, despair never arrives as the response to it all.

The Absurd is the philosophical framework left behind by Camus throughout both his fictional and critical writing. Contained within it are the suggestions of existentialism, realism, and logical positivism, but with an empowering pursuit despite a gloomy social order. *The Plague* defines it quite well—the absurd is the permanent state of affairs to which all must admit and embrace; the endeavor to assign meaning to the meaningless, the attempt to know the unknowable, a world without God. Camus was writing this novel amid World War II, during which he was a leading voice for the French Resistance and deeply affected by the abundant suffering at the hands of tyrants. His banquet speech upon receiving the Nobel Prize in 1957 elucidates the call of the writer to bear the "misery and the hope" endured by the current generation living through the chronicle of history. On this point, critics argue the story is merely an allegory to the sweeping fascism of the time, but even if so, Camus accomplishes a feat beyond it. Whereas the misery can be found at every turn of the page, hope is muffled between the lines in how to grapple with the endless loops of hours and days prolonged by nature.

The lethal disease drags time along with it. Monotony sets in and the empty habits of the townspeople are now accompanied only by their insipid, muffled sounds. Enter Tarrou, a visitor to Oran, with his journal entry on how to wrestle with relativity:

> *"Query: How contrive not to waste one's time? Answer. By being fully aware of it all the while. Ways in which this can be done: By spending one's days on an uneasy chair in a dentist's waiting room; by remaining on one's balcony all a Sunday afternoon; by listening to lectures in a language one doesn't know; by travelling by the longest and least convenient train routes, and of course standing all the way; by queueing at the box office of theatres and then not booking a seat. And so forth."*

Above is a passage with the first invocation of irony as a near neighbor to the absurd. The pointlessness to the chores is straightforward, clearly irrational, and yet the resulting insight is of some assistance. It offers the awareness of time in return, and the understanding of how society rejects to partake in burdens resembling a parody. Akin to how precise behavior can be achieved from imprecise knowledge, the irrational can yield prudent results. Absurdism requires a surrender to an underlying reality beneath the veneer of normalcy, and the occupying space below, therefore, contains a swath of opposites and asymmetries that reveal doorways to other senses of being, those of which are not immediately apparent in routine phenomenology.

Of Loss

Naturally, with a plague ravaging the town, there is much to grieve. Suffering is a ubiquitous actor, taking victims regardless of peacetime or war. On deck to alleviate the resulting emotional torment is an assignment of which humans are awfully fond: to uncover some type of meaning or purpose to explain everything. It is in our nature to desire and know the ends behind events. Otherwise, incentives are nonexistent in any causation-based schema, which just happens to be the foundation of life itself. A reason must exist for why we water flowers, for instance, otherwise it would just be strange behavior. When applied to existence as a concept, especially upon the realization that none of us asked to be here in the first place, to invoke this can create a minefield of rabbit holes, and a devotion to crafted explanations rather than honest ones.

Seldom does fiction eventually become reality. Where *The Plague* truly becomes penetratingly stark and sobering are the eerie relatable illustrations to the present moment as the lethal disease surges through the dreary evenings of Oran. The minds of the residents are trapped clinging to destiny and the eternal, but are forced to concede their role as a mere passenger, looking out from their homes to the empty streets where the shrilling of the wind carries the hollow sound of their fear:

> *"Thus, in a middle course between these heights and depths, they drifted through life rather than lived, the prey of aimless days and sterile memories, like wandering shadows that could have acquired substance only by consenting to root themselves in the solid earth of their distress. Thus, too, they came to know the incorrigible sorrow of all prisoners and exiles, which is to live in company with a memory that serves no purpose. Even the past, of which they thought incessantly, had a savour only of regret..."*

The trains are no longer running, and every hotel porter, businessman, and bartender have only their thoughts as solace to contemplate their new role as prey. The presence of an active predator conjures those pits of uncertainty and agony concerning our place in the cosmos, but they seem to be less dark and harrowing when a meaning is assigned to describe reality. Dr. Rieux, the quiet hero of the novel and a reflection of Camus himself, maintains "common decency" as his act of defiance, with an understanding of the predicament that cements his focus and sense of duty to the ill. Although it is his job to see life fade, he has never been able to get used to people dying. Finality affects us all and cannot be avoided. Father Paneloux— the priest of the town—serves as the mouthpiece for the teleological stance on the cataclysm. The problem of evil is dealt with cleanly throughout his interactions with Rieux, but mostly in his sermon in which he delivers a postulation that if an omnibenevolent destiny is the nature of life, then there is no need to grumble when evil strikes. Rieux keeps responsibility ahead of him and tries to save those affected, whilst Tarrou resists this message with stoic enmity. What interests him is being a saint, and an idea at the heart of his resolve, articulated in one of the most memorable passages from the novel. "All I maintain," Tarrou says, "is that on this earth there are pestilences and there are victims, and it's up to us, so far as possible, not to join forces with the pestilences."

We are result-seeking creatures, and yet we cannot know the culmination of our actions while on earth. There are commitments we must execute in the face of plagues, which vary in form and are certainly not limited to a lethal virus as Camus demonstrates. It is always in the face of loss in which we must recognize these obligations, in fidelity to those who are taken in death's swoop. Within the absurdity of tragedies performed by nature and the ambiguity of existence, however, lies a landscape of individual features of inspiration, each containing the idiosyncratic wherewithal to be enjoyed for its own sake.

Of Love

Our striving contains numerous, fulfilling experiences while attempting to make sense of life. With the pointlessness of the world as a given, according to Camus, the nature of being is unknowable given our current cognitive constraints. Forced to abandon asking questions of "why" upon observation of these constructed societies, it is imperative to ask how to flourish in existence. We are then called upon to fill in the arcane gaps between how we live and why we do so. To live in the absurd exponentially increases the value of those pleasures that endlessly enthrall us—conversations about what we believe, great food with great company, enduring friendships, the moral choice, the right action. All the while we remain in combat with the dichotomy between purpose and purposelessness. Granting ourselves positions as the architects to this map of understanding, we can engage with life in a way that is deeper than any outcome-based explanation. Conversations, for instance, are catalysts for laughter as well as vital to our personal decryption of honorable virtues. They are ubiquitous throughout our lives and yet each one has something new to offer, and something new to learn. A world that prioritizes the intrinsic value contained within these experiences would be of greater value as it would hone in on performing actions for purely their sake rather than an external reward.

Camus is appreciated for the infusion of love in his writing. It may not manifest itself boldly while reading *The Plague*, but it is there, as soft beams of sunlight, and allied by his appreciation for life. A few occupants of Oran, including Raymond Raybert, have been unlucky in their geographical placement at the time when catastrophe hits. He is a journalist who cannot purge an exigent need to break out and see the woman he loves. Escape plans are drawn up and the necessary insiders are befriended. To be locked down broaches a new feeling of enchantment, perhaps even fixation, with those we cannot live without. Raybert is clearly enamored by the love of his life, but eventually his infatuation and attention turn elsewhere—to a noble cause in the fight against the plague.

As many characters demonstrate in *The Plague*, people are not the sole recipients of affection. There is love in progress, intentions, and in sacrifice. The call to arms requires us to direct all our love, hope, and meaning to the cryptic rather than the certain. To marvel and engage in the experience of striving. Uncomfortable as it may be, this way of living comes without regard to the finish line. The climber who attempts to summit a mountain that never ceases to grow in altitude. The diver wanting to touch the bottom of the ocean that continuously grows deeper. This intention can be seen as a losing struggle since these moments themselves are fleeting. Although it can be perceived as irrational, this existentialist point of view is the outlook on life that grants the most autonomy. This expedition provides a process for always improving our navigation through life's problems and the contemplation of our place in the universe. Existence asks us to be content with the unknown. Unnerving by way of appearance, this very well could be the remedy that keeps us sane.

In *The Plague*, Camus reminds us of the uniting (yet grim) truth that we are all destined for the same end. And this is the case whether a pandemic is sweeping the planet or not. When it is, the mutual fate of every planetary cohabitant can be seen all too clearly. Distractions melt away. We are confined to limited space relying on our own minds for company, seemingly without an escape. The same is true of existence itself. The plague reduces us to our bare purpose— to exist and then to die. As we endure these long months of isolation as calamity strikes outside of our doors, a worthwhile reflection is that our own mortality does not have to be deemed the darkest crumb of truth. What is real and undeniable is intrinsically precious and benefits the plight of society. It's steadying, and promotes an incendiary reaction to live as well as we can.

There will come a time when our own plague will meet its vaccine, and we will have curtailed its spread. It is precisely these moments of perceived calmness in which we would do well to be extra wary, extra circumspect of the distance between what is and what seems. In the closing pages of his celebrated novel, Camus writes of a resumed life of negation for the citizens of Oran. The French epigram by Jean-Baptiste Alphonse Karr is, therefore, essential to keep in one's pocket. It reads: *plus ça change, plus c'est la même chose*—the more things change, the more they stay the same.

"Calmly they denied, in the teeth of the evidence, that we have ever known a crazy world in which men were killed off like flies, or that precise savagery, that calculated frenzy of the plague, which instilled an odious freedom as to all that was not the here and now; or those charnel-housed stenches which stupified whom they did not kill. In short, they denied that we had ever been that hag-ridden populace a part of which was daily fed into a furnace and went up in oily fumes, while the rest, in shackled impotence, waited their turn."

.

MIRRORS OF SHADOWS

Words and their perennial utility

A VARIETY OF MEDIUMS EXIST WITH THE ABILITY TO ELEVATE words to a new height. Speeches provide the atmosphere of attention and importance, music and film cause the emotional senses to swell, and psychological "highs" are sculpted thanks to the encroachments of smarmy entertainment platforms to keep the concentration of consumers. However flashy and seductively conducted, very often forgotten and left behind is the origin behind all of these forms. Long before any final cut is always a "blank page".

Walter Benjamin has to be the most prolific collector of quotations according to his reputation. All of us do the same, whether unconsciously or consciously, as fragments of wisdom take their place in a memorable assembly of words in an essay snippet, sonnet excerpt, song lyric, or a closing remark in a speech. Prose never fades in the chronicle of history whereas the forms it takes will. Performances will not matter. But the messages contained within most certainly will, and always be passively awaiting the next solitary reader of history. The remaining embodiment will always be what was composed, penned flat on a scroll of pages, adamant and resolute, locked in a capsule with the soul of the author.

Technology can be mainly accredited with the drop in utility of words and language. The digital age gives the appearance that it will never yield back its ground as innovation is in the process of gradually crowding out the sacred elements of being human. Edgar Allen Poe once said, "Words have no power to impress the mind *without the exquisite horror of their reality*". This echoes Nietzsche as well who once quipped that all he needed was something to write with and a sheet of paper to turn the world upside down. These sentiments are held by two men who valiantly proved the passion and robustness of the written word. Far from dormant, words in it of themselves contain idiosyncratic properties of weight and meaning. The new knowledge of this fact is no longer anecdotal, but scientific.

The research of Dr. Lera Boroditsky and her team have been studying truly wonderful insights in the field of linguistics. The leading vehicle to transmit knowledge from one to another has about 7,000 variations across the world. These are disappearing, as it seems with everything valuable nowadays, at a rate of one language per week. To illustrate the preciseness in communication, Lera and her team give a few prominent examples with the benefit of new scientific data. In Russian, for instance, there is not a catch-all term for the color blue. Russian speakers have to constantly differentiate between light and dark shades of blue. When analyzing the brains of both Russian and English speakers, it was discovered that Russian speakers were quicker to discern the shifting colors aided by an ignited categorical reaction in the brain when the colors would alternate. No such alarm was set off in the brains of English speakers.

A far-reaching concept in other languages other than English is the gender association for specific nouns. Dr. Boroditsky uses the example of the word "bridge" which is grammatically feminine in German but grammatically masculine in Spanish. Upon asking speakers of both languages, Germans are more likely to associate bridges with stereotypically feminine descriptions such as "beautiful" or "elegant" where the Spanish refer to them as "strong", stereotypically masculine. The same can be said of the sun and the moon, which share opposite gender associations.

Perhaps the most consequential finding from the research is on causation. Dr. Boroditsky gives the example of a vase accidently knocked over and broken. Non-English languages would communicate that "The vase broke," rather than "He broke the vase," even if somebody was involved in tipping the pillar over. Upon showing two sets of speakers the same accident, it was found that English speakers were more likely to remember who caused the accident, while Spanish speakers more often remembered *the fact that it was an accident.* This perfectly fits with the West's obsession with blame, and it also has tremendous implications in the court of law. All of the previous findings are an incitement to use language with the utmost precision and intent. Everything that occurs in history not only requires, but deserves, an appropriate depiction that can be permanently placed in textbooks, journals, and newspapers for future generations to fully access the gravity of moments of the past.

This is a responsibility that cannot afford a great shortfall. *"The world is at least half terrible,"* as Maggie Smith wrote in her poem "Good Bones". And as Camus illuminated in his Nobel speech, a writer is not "in the service of those who make history; *he is at the service of those who suffer it."* The world functions better when we can use language to match the severity of things. The written word is the underdog for these moments, but it is a unifying instrument capable of igniting rhapsodic senses and compassion. The result of this, if done correctly, should be to equate the gravity of the moment to corresponding solemnity, acuity, and profundity in the language used. To match the grievance with an illustration of words is a feat which should be brimming with examples, and yet the premier successes are much more on the side of rare. This is essence of Poe's musing, and in order to invoke him once more, a tour down the most revolting moments in history are often necessary to gain a glimpse of proper reflection and sentiment.

The scene in Iraq of July 1979 was the genesis to decades of abject terror for Iraqi citizens. Suddam Hussein deposed al-Bakr, took over as president, and could not even wait a week to call a meeting of the Ba'ath party to vanquish his enemies. In a room resembling a small and smoky theater, the Iraqi people became subject to a one-party state with a lethal ruler, and families fell to their knees not in praise but because of their new captivity. Coercion of the foulest kind which is difficult even to write.

While giving a speech Christopher Hitchens once sonorously described an experience near a mass grave in the south of Iraq as the closest he could portray the evil of the Baa'th regime. Mass graves were the heedless trenches used for the bodies of hundreds of state executions. During an excavation of one of these pits, the wind picked up. Eventually all observers were covered, head to foot, in the ashes of the victims. These were brutal murder victims of innocent Arabs, Kurds, Turkmen, Yazidis, Armenians, and more Iraqi people. Those who had been threatened to fall in line with the oppression at the threat of having to watch the execution of their family. This type of evil, as Hitchens stated, is the kind that destroys itself. It is the type too vile to be worthy of the same classification that the word provides for other domains.

Another contender in this effort would be Viktor Frankel. He was a prisoner in Auschwitz and lived to tell the tale, unlike many of the men and women he encountered. He is awarded the title of founder for the psychoanalysis method known as logotherapy, a practice of which he developed during his time in the Nazi concentration camps and was of great aid to fellow inmates. In his chronicle on the experience, *Man's Search for Meaning,* Frankel writes of a restless night. Looking around the barracks, he noticed several friends shaking in their sleep, supposedly due to a nightmare. The thought that came to him was annihilating, and of destitute sorrow. Frankel could not bring himself to wake them up. He knew that whatever they were dreaming could not be worse than the reality they were living.

Notice how dreams are conceptually full of infinite possibilities, and Frankel uses this comparison to arrive at the *limitless* property to the range of imagination. The idea that a slice of reality, of history, was so incomprehensible to endure that imagination itself could not conjure a comparable experience contains a weight heavy enough that should bring anyone who contemplates its intensity to collapse. Every word matters and carries value that substitutes cannot offer. Perhaps if occurrences had the correct language around it, we could begin to care about the right things rather than the convenient ones.

Language can do more than just wait for the right reader. It can spur a riot with a new one, appear unavoidable to more. It has the reaction of immediacy and can command attention elsewhere. Words are scrawled across billions of platforms and pages throughout one's lifetime, and although it is an arduous undertaking to parse and consume it all, language is the only unwavering means of conveying knowledge and interpreting the world through life and the centuries. Due to its constancy, the impression that most writing just ends up on dusty bookshelves has to put in its rightful, anachronistic place. Benjamin Franklin once wrote about the oral sermons of Reverend Whitefield, who delivered impassioned, fierce, and notable speeches. Preaching might have to be afterwards explained or qualified, he said, but *"the written word shall remain."* It gladly shall, closely followed by the responsibility to treasure and preserve it, and the room for freedom of expression. Here's to its enduring health, and the astounding personal nature despite the capability of its global reach.

PANORAMA

Fellwalkers by day and night

THE FIRST CONTRADICTION THAT TRULY STRUCK ME AS A puzzle worth examining was the logical problem of evil. Time went on and more started to appear with a similar paradoxical flavor. As a reminder that we live in an unbalanced world, riddled by this misdirecting fog, I keep an ongoing list of incongruities: The labor of many years over a work of art can be enjoyed in minutes, buildings are named after those who never built them, when songs of love evoke pain, the dying have the most to teach us about living, churches hold both marriages and funerals, the reason we laugh at the wrong thing is because we know what the right thing is, how one's mind can be the loudest when sitting in silence, the smartest inventions are built for the most dangerous men to use, and fighting for peace by means of war.

The realities of these can give the impression that we are all vagabonds in a wilderness that never quite ends, or rather—never ceases to confuse. I have noticed, over time, that the presence of these asymmetries and dualities are invariably contrasted by moments of seemingly intangible clarity. Occurrences of this breed are the ones that are never fully understood but are immediately recognizable. The height of these moments can sometimes only be attributable to a spiritual delirium of some kind. They stand opposed to all the chaos swirling around in the subconscious, and suddenly, all physiological and cognitive senses are oriented perfectly and calibrated to maximum fulfillment. The instants are rare—when all cosmic forces seem to be in line, time collapses, and your mind floats aloft, on a higher plane of experience.

The razor-sharp art critic John Berger writes of a strain of this transcendent state in his brilliant book of critiques, *About Looking*. In the final essay, he writes of a field near his flat. There are two ways he could venture home. The first is via the main road with considerable traffic and noise, and the other is a side road that leads to a level crossing. When the crossing is closed, the angle between the railway lines affords a view of the vast field previously mentioned, and he is able to pause here and look out into the distance. Why doesn't he walk through the field itself? It affords him considerable pleasure, after all, and is not out of his way. He replies:

"It is a question of contingencies overlapping. The events which take place in the field—two birds chasing one another, a cloud crossing the sun and changing the colour of the green—acquire a special significance because they occur during the minute or two during which I am obliged to wait. It is as though these minutes fill a certain area of time which exactly fits the spatial area of the field. Time and space conjoin."

Forever will we be chained to juxtapositions. As in the excerpt above, and with many of these psychological experiences, the dichotomy is between that of a spectator and participant. Fields of experience can alter at once. The very same confusing terrain can suddenly morph into a landscape completely in sync with everything perfectly in place. Navigating this is the struggle we all face and merely the fate of the human condition, but its composure is more malleable than it may seem.

As I write this, I am sure of only one thing—a thunderous idea by that leveling, percipient French writer from the prior pages. Life will surely not offer any redeeming sense of coherence in the future. Equilibrium between *what is* and what *should be* is always in flux. But within the battle of balancing the world is the presence of everything worth fighting for, which is no accident. The state of combatting harmony against chaos is a perpetual one, which brings me to the seven words by Camus on how one ought to respond:

In order to exist, man must rebel.

Meanwhile, the ironies of life play on. In our own odyssey of triumphs and failings, of laughter and teardrops, of longings and actualities, there is much to consider and suggest. Be concerned with suffering and wary of those who aren't. Fend off all simple explanations in a complex world. Take on striving towards impossibilities. Point at those who exploit credulity. Always try to identify hidden ethical imperatives. Consider the cosmic. Never forget that the *mot juste* must be stitched with the motive to honor and impel. And finally—keep a constant watch to recognize the necessary and worthwhile rebellions, and engage in them if you can, before the curtain falls.

"But to stand in the midst of this *rerun concordia discors* (discordant harmony of things) and the whole marvelous uncertainty and ambiguity of existence without questioning, without trembling with the craving and rapture of questioning, without at least hating the person who questions, perhaps even being faintly amused by him — I feel to be contemptible."

—Nietzsche, *The Gay Science*

"Everything great is just as difficult to realize as it is rare to find."

—Spinoza, *Ethics*

Made in the USA
Middletown, DE
27 July 2021